THE
CHRISTIAN HERITAGE
IN AMERICA

By GEORGE HEDLEY

NEW YORK
THE MACMILLAN COMPANY
1947

PRINTED IN THE UNITED STATES OF AMERICA
BY THE VAIL-BALLOU PRESS, INC., BINGHAMTON, N. Y.

The army that is the Church of Jesus Christ is one drawn from all the miscellany of humankind, and each division of it has its own proud traditions and its own special qualities. We belong to one division or to another as we may have been recruited, or as we may have chosen to enlist. A few of us may decide to seek reassignment to another division, because we think we belong more naturally to it and therefore shall serve more effectively in its ranks. That is a secondary matter.

The important thing is that we are all in the same army. We fight against the same foemen: hate, and cruelty, and evil in its every form. We seek to obey the same commands of love to God and love to fellow man. Within our forces we endeavor to hold the unity of the spirit in the bond of peace. Knowing this, believing in it, living by it, we rejoice as we hear the battle-cry of each advancing unit of our forces.

(See below, p. 113.)

The army that is the Church of Jesus Christ is one drawn from all the miscellany of humankind, and each division of it has its own proud traditions and its own special qualities. We belong to one division or to another as we may have been recruited, or as we may have chosen to enlist. A few of us may decide to seek reassignment to another division, because we think we belong more naturally to it and therefore shall serve more effectively in its ranks. That is a secondary matter.

The important thing is that we are all in the same army. We fight against the same foeman bare, and cruelty, and evil in its every form. We seek to obey the same commands of love to God and love to fellow man. Within our forces we endeavour to hold the unity of the spirit in the bond of peace...Knowing this, believing in it, living by it, we rejoice as we hear the battle-cry of each advancing unit of our forces.

(See below, p. 115.)

viii FOREWORD

Mills College

FOREWORD

THE substance of the following pages derives from sermons recently preached in the Chapel of Mills College. The student Chapel Committee, as is its wont, selected the general theme; and the student body by its background and character determined the manner of approach. To the students, therefore, go my primary thanks.

Two studies have been added to those prepared for the Chapel: that dealing with Eastern Orthodoxy and that treating of American revivalism. They are necessary to the historic picture, but lie outside the range of interest and acquaintance of the average Mills student. I have not attempted to discuss the more decisive departures from the general pattern, such as Mormonism and Christian Science. As yet they are derivatives of, rather than contributory to, the main stream of American Christianity; and their stories are so complex as to require exhaustive treatment if any.

I am grateful to the Mills College *Weekly* for permission to reprint those parts of a few of the studies which appeared in its columns, and to the editors and publishers of *The Christian Register* for similar permission to re-use materials from the essay on liberal Christianity. Biblical quotations are from the version of 1611 (AV), except in a very few cases where I have used my own renderings of the text (GH).

The quest has been one amid diversity from and toward essential unity. I pray that it has not transgressed liberty nor failed in charity.

G. H.

Mills College
St. Barnabas' Day
1945

CONTENTS

CONTENTS

THE CHRISTIAN HERITAGE
IN AMERICA

I

'WHOSE GOD IS THE LORD'
(The Jews)

'Blessed is the nation whose God is the Lord.'
—Psalm 33:12 (AV).

'Spiritually we are Semites.'—Pope Pius XII, A.D. 1942.

THE story of American Christianity begins at the eastern end of the Mediterranean. There, compressed between the desert and the sea, lies a little land about a hundred miles long by thirty to forty miles wide, which never can have supported a population more numerous than the million or so persons who now live there. Its natural resources are limited, its commerce is and always has been negligible, its military potentialities are nil. It is nevertheless in our culture the best known land of antiquity: best known in both senses of the word, in that of thoroughness and in that of favorable judgment.

Home of few more than a million people at any one time, Palestine today is 'The Holy Land' for not less than eight hundred thirty-six million human souls: for six hundred million Christians, for two hundred twenty-one million Muslims, and for over fifteen million, scattered among the nations and infiltrating all, who hold primary right in the tradition because they count and call them-

I

selves Jews. Producers of a minimum of surviving native literature (totalling a thousand pages in English print), Palestine and her people have occasioned and inspired the filling of innumerable libraries. Never herself a potent factor in the fluctuations of warfare and of politics, the little Mediterranean community has influenced the thinking and affected the actions of leaders and rulers all over the world.

Despite the great and vital contributions of Palestine to western culture, that people which stems most directly from Palestine has been treated with something other than eager affection: has been subjected, not only in the past but with renewed fury in our own day, to bitter opposition and to fierce brutality. Anti-Semitism was a Nazi dogma, but it has long been also a general European habit. There is reason to believe that it has been and is a recognizable American tendency. We face thus a situation in which many, if not most, of those who owe the wellsprings of their own culture to the Jews, violently repudiate their debt and hold in contempt the tradition by which nevertheless they still are controlled.

This manifestly is an absurd situation. With Hitler it became a tragic one. In our own land it is a dangerous one. Even among persons of good will there is less of specific knowledge, and therefore less of positive appreciation, than is needed effectively to ward off anti-Semitism in one's self and to counter it in others. Yet every Christian is inescapably Jewish, since Christianity sprang from Jewish roots and ever has been nourished by Jewish streams. What are some of the things that being Jewish involves?

To clear the decks for action, it is well to remind ourselves that being Jewish is not in any significant degree a biological matter. There is no Jewish 'race.' There is no clearly identifiable blood strain, no recognizable physical type, which belongs inclusively and exclusively to the Jewish people. The Hebrews were Arabs to begin with, and their original heredity is that of all the peoples of the desert and the fertile crescent. Through the centuries their descendants were increasingly mixed with other peoples, Semitic and non-Semitic alike (and of course they *are* alike, as any anthropologist will testify). The years of exile and of dispersion increased the admixture from still other, more distant groups. The Jew is identifiable not by appearance but by ideas, not in features but in faith. What is a Jew? A Jew is anyone who considers himself Jewish. Beyond that, a Jew is anyone who shares Jewish attitudes and judgments, whether or not he knows or admits their origin.

And so all Christians are Jewish. Three major strands in Jewish tradition, resulting in three major values of human experience, have entered into the standard pattern of our western, so-called 'Christian,' world. One of these strands comes from the early Israelite and Jewish prophets, one from the priesthood which later assumed leadership, one from the apocalyptists who fought the rearguard action in defence of Jewish national and cultural integrity. The prophets sounded the cry for social justice. The priests asserted the duties of humble reverence. The apocalyptists uttered the declarations of unconquerable faith and the vows of absolute loyalty.

The prophets were spokesmen for the ordinary man in the relationships of his ordinary life. Amos challenged the inequities which had arisen out of agricultural settlement and developing political complexity. Micah protested the concentration of financial control in the metropolis. Isaiah condemned the arrogance and brutality of his own fellows in the upper strata of Jerusalem society. Jeremiah pled for quietness and contentment as against military ambition. Nahum applauded the fall of Assyria's greedy imperialism, Habakkuk foresaw the inevitable collapse of Alexander's.

These men were politicians all: the stump speakers and political pamphleteers of their place and time. Dealing with what we call secular things, they dealt with them in a deeply religious spirit: that is to say, in a spirit of profound concern and of complete devotion. Thus it befell that political evaluation in terms of human welfare and of elementary justice became part of the religious pattern of Israel and Judah; and thus that the prophets' insistence on the wellbeing of men and women became a standard element (if one not always realized) in the religious living of that offshoot of Judaism called Christianity.

Less applauded in our own time, less understood ever, but not less important either in their day or in ours, are the priests who administered the formal ceremonies of the Jerusalem *cultus*. They were assailed by the prophets as being guilty of formalism, of selfishness, of hypocrisy. They have been discounted more recently by those who see no point in ritual rules other than the specific ones which they themselves take for granted. Nevertheless the priests long guided Jewish life, and they alone kept it living. That life which they preserved, and which they did so much to fashion, lives on in our usages and judgments today.

The key word in Jewish ritual is 'holiness.' At its earlier and lower levels this 'holiness' represented a kind of taboo. Certain places must not be entered, certain objects must not be touched, certain names must not be pronounced. In a higher range 'holiness' came to connote moral as well as physical purity and perfection. The reverence of the ritual thus was understood to express an inward reverence toward the highest values of life.

This ritual, and the sanctuaries in which it was enshrined, literally saved Judaism from extinction when the Jewish kingdom was liquidated in the sixth century B.C. Lacking the visible symbols of political identity, the populace had left to them no sign of their oneness save the ceremonies of the temple and the household. These the priests preserved and emphasized, and therein they kept alight the gleam of Jewish faith and hope.

Through all the succeeding years, even though the Jerusalem temple was destroyed again and finally, and though the priesthood as an order vanished, the solemn forms which the priests had taught availed to keep the Jewish people Jews. Those forms, and no less their vitalizing inner spirit, incipient Christianity took over as a matter of course. The standard Christian Sunday service reproduces the usage of the ancient Synagogue: singing and prayers, the reading of the Scripture and its interpretation.

There is, alas!, no moment in the Protestant service quite comparable to that in the Synagogue, when the tabernacle is opened and the sacred roll of the law is lifted from its place to be read to the congregation. Protestants as a community are not old enough to care or to value so much. On the other hand, what Protestantism does have of order and respect, and furthermore what it has in the glory of the ancient writings themselves, exists because the Jews created it.

Out of the dark days of national collapse and cultural bitterness rose yet a third authentic, unconquerable Jewish voice. Those writers known as the apocalyptists wrote in code, for they could not speak openly in the hearing of the royal or imperial police. But the code was clear to them who were meant to understand it, and it is clear for us through historical comprehension and personal participation. Through all of the fantastic visions, through all of the cryptic numerology, there rings the voice of the conquered who would not admit defeat. 'We may suffer,' they chanted, 'but we are on God's side: and so at the last we shall triumph. We may be despised and oppressed; we may be beaten, imprisoned, silenced, slain: but the truth of the ages is ours, and our truth at the last will prevail.'

Some readers will remember Franz Werfel's play *The Eternal Road*. In it is apocalyptic *redivivus:* the stubborn loyalty, the undying devotion, the triumphant faith of those who know that affliction is testing, that humiliation is learning, that defeat may be transmuted into victory. No other people of mankind has been tested, so fiercely so long, as has this people of Israel whose God is the Lord. No other people has shown such survival power, for no other has had such survival value.

From the very beginning the Christian community shared in the spirit, and adopted the literary devices, of these indestructible devotees of the truth into which they had been born. The New Testament book of Revelation, the supreme consolation of Christian martyrs in every century, is from the literary point of view a *mélange* of earlier Jewish apocalyptic writings. 'The glorious company of the apostles, the noble army of martyrs,' praise not only the Lord God Almighty, but also these Jewish heroes who along the eternal road have maintained their conviction, their allegiance, their devotion.

At the head of this chapter stands the dictum of His Holiness Pope Pius XII to the effect that 'spiritually we are Semites.' For a Nazi to hate and to destroy Jewish men and women was a violation of human decency. For a Christian to abjure his spiritual descent, to despise those who created and those who share his spiritual heritage, is a violation of all historic truth and all spiritual value. We Christians are Jewish, whether we like it or not. And why should we not like it?

Shall we not like, and accept, and obey, the moral imperative of the Jewish prophets? The worth of men and women in their own right is the basic criterion in the Christian scale of values. It is the criterion assumed and asserted and used by that late North Israelite prophet whom we call Our Lord. It is the criterion, the only criterion, by whose using life may become for all of us decent, and creative, and free. It is a Jewish criterion: Jewish in its origins, Jewish in its maintenance through all the years that have passed since first it was enunciated. It cannot but be accepted if human life is to have meaning; and in so far as we accept it, we are Jewish.

Shall we not like, and accept, and follow, the reverential practice of the Jewish priesthood? The tragic weakness of today is casualness, sloppiness, non-recognition of ultimate values. The corrective is available, in appreciation of what the past has given us and in humble acknowledgement that we on our part have given but little. Form indeed may be deadly when it is not understood, when it is not inwardly apprehended. Form is assurance, and strength, and stability, when its meaning is grasped and its power used. We bow our heads to pray, and it means something. We stand to praise, and that means something too. If these practices mean nothing to us, we are not Jewish; and we are not Christian; and we are not quite alive.

Shall we not like and accept, finally, the loyal faith of the Jewish apocalyptists? The major lack of recent American life has been suffering. We have paid relatively little for the treasures that are ours, and so we are tempted to value them little. Our brothers and sisters in Europe, our brothers and cousins and sweethearts in the armed forces, in these years have been paying much: and on our account. They could not continue to pay the price unless they believed, unless they were sustained by that triumphant conviction which inspired the Jewish Daniel in Babylon, the Jewish John on Patmos.

'Blessed is the nation whose God is the Lord.' Blessed be the nation which has given us so much: which has given us the ideal of human dignity; which has given us the usage of human reverence; which has given us the challenge of human devotion. Few of us are acquainted with the Jewish tradition at first hand. Each of us is indebted to it, well-nigh has been created by it. And so the case is rested with those words which denote the immemorial loyalty and faith of all who are Jewish: 'Hear, O Israel; the Lord our God—the Lord is one.'

II

'YE SHALL KNOW THE TRUTH'

(The Orthodox)

'Ye shall know the truth, and the truth shall make you free.'
—St. John 8:32 (AV).

'This is life eternal, that they might know thee the only true God, and Jesus Christ whom thou hast sent.'
—St. John 17:3 (AV).

OF ALL the major traditions of Christendom, the least numerously represented in the American community is the Eastern Orthodox. It is therefore the least known by Americans, the least direct in its effect upon American life. A few specific items from the Eastern heritage, rescued by the Tractarians of the last century, now are in fairly general use as hymns and prayers. But while the average American Protestant has attended a few Roman Catholic services, at least a wedding or a funeral, he does not know where the local Greek or Russian Church is and has no thought of finding out.

Liberal Christians have come to challenge some of the original emphases of historic Protestantism, but have maintained for it real respect and deep affection. Roman Catholicism they have seen from outside, and as Protestants long have distrusted; so that only in recent years, and only in part, has liberal tolerance been broadened to include the Catholic pattern within its area of good will. Eastern Orthodoxy the western world has not known at first hand, has thought of very little, seldom has regarded as a significant aspect of the total Christian tradition.

Nevertheless the Eastern Churches: Greek, Russian, Armenian, Coptic, Syrian, Rumanian, Bulgarian: are organizationally as old as that of Rome, and temperamentally are the least of all altered since the earliest days of Christian history. When we come to an enquiry into Catholicism, we shall find our type sentence in a third-century dictum of St. Cyprian, and for Protestantism in a declaration of the sixteenth-century Martin Luther. For Eastern Orthodoxy we must turn back to the New Testament, for the Eastern Churches always have been there.

The Fourth Gospel, written in Ephesus and seeking to present the Christian faith within the categories of Platonist and Stoic philosophy, is at once the authentic product of Eastern Christianity and the continuing fountainhead of its inspiration. Rome preferred the vigorous, objective narrative of St. Mark and the vivid pictures of the Johannine Revelation. The East was better pleased, and fully content, with the quiet mysticism of what St. Clement of Alexandria called 'a spiritual gospel.' By a happy compromise (though after not a little of controversy) the imperial Church in the fourth century decided to recognize and preserve, and so the twentieth century has available, the major documents of both traditions.

The first and foremost value among those which the East has stressed appears in the very name of Eastern Christianity. 'Ortho-doxy' is 'right teaching'; and truth ever has been the primary quest of Eastern Christians. The equivalent but richer Greek word, *aletheia*, rings through the Ephesian Gospel. 'Ye shall know the truth, and the truth shall make you free,' promises the incarnate Word who himself is 'the true light come into the world.' Jesting Pilate asks, 'What is truth?,' and the Church devotes herself to seeking and stating the answer.

This eagerness for knowledge of ultimate reality of course is a direct inheritance from the intellectual adventuring of a still earlier Greece. Conversion to Christianity did not destroy, did not significantly change, the intellectual concern of men who had been brought up to enquire and to think. The authors of the Fourth Gospel and of the Epistle to the Hebrews were the first, but by no means the last, to bring together Christian inspiration and Greek illumination. After them Justin the Martyr, trained in the Greek philosophical schools, found for himself the true philosophy in Christianity, and proceeded thereupon to expound Christianity in truly philosophic terms. After him again came the three great Christian Platonists of the catechetical school in Alexandria: Pantaenus, St. Clement, and Origen.

Thus before the end of the third Christian century the Eastern Churches had produced a tremendous body of trenchant philosophical writing; and within it not a little of that intellectual formulation which has remained the common possession of all Christians ever since. But since these men were concerned to pursue truth, they were driven of necessity to identify and to abjure what they considered to be error. Thus there developed, and again in full harmony with the habit of ancient Greece, a second major characteristic of Eastern Christian thought: that of definition.

The very mention of 'orthodoxy,' 'right teaching,' infers the existence of its opposite: 'heterodoxy,' or 'other teaching.' It is possible to be cynical about such a demarcation, to say (for example) that 'orthodoxy is my doxy, and heterodoxy is your doxy.' The fact remains that the distinction between truth and falsehood is real and crucial for anyone who cares about knowing the truth. The Eastern Church did thus care, and therefore the Eastern Church proceeded sharply and critically to define.

The consequence was the series of the great Councils of the Church, from that of Nicaea in the early fourth century onward, each of them discussing a critical point of Christian doctrine and each issuing in a formal declaration of the position agreed upon by the majority of the clerics assembled. Liberals in an anti-intellectual mood sometimes have poked fun at the minutiae of the distinctions debated, notably at the disputes and the ultimate excommunications (and, indirectly, even the bloodshed) over the single-letter difference between *homoousion*, 'same essence,' and *homooiousion*, 'similar essence.' Such humor is ill-placed and ill-directed. Had no decision been made at Nicaea, Christianity inevitably would have disintegrated into innumerable petty philosophical sects, no one of them adequate to survive the strenuous, contentious, bewildering days of the reorganization of the Empire. Had the wrong decision been made: that is, had Arius prevailed in his contention that God and the *Logos* were separate and disparate rather than one and indivisible: in all probability the same disintegration ultimately would have occurred.

We cannot talk about truth without using words; nor

can we talk about truth usefully unless we use words sharply, decisively, significantly. To say that philosophical discussion is irrelevant to life is to say that life has for us no meaning that matters. Not even the Epicureans, not even the original Cynics, went so far as this. Christianity ever has insisted that life does have meaning: that life has ultimate, everlasting meaning for everyone who lives. It follows that the Christian must seek to understand that meaning, and therefore that he must strive honestly and specifically to define it. Theological disputation is not a pastime for leisurely professors, and certainly it is not a trivial amusement for anyone. Theological clarity is the necessary foundation for any reputable sort of thinking about life. Theological conviction thus becomes the necessary impetus for consistent and unwearying devotion in life.

It is precisely because the Church in the Eastern Mediterranean lands began by caring about the truth, and proceeded by defining the truth as sharply as her best minds could achieve, that through all these centuries she has exhibited the third characteristic that must be noticed: the characteristic of continuance. In general the East is less impressed by the time factor than are we in the West; and the Eastern Church exhibits her timelessness now and then in ways that seem to us ludicrous if not positively annoying. One recalls the worries of the Anglican Canon in Jerusalem who tried annually to make up a schedule of the Holy Week services of the various Eastern communions, for the information and convenience of the tourists of the season. Too polite to give the Canon a flat 'No,' the patriarch and the archimandrites seem to have mentioned any time that happened to come into their heads; but not in the author's experience during two spring festival seasons in Palestine did a service begin at the precise time which the good Canon's time-table showed. Either nothing was happening in the Church at all, or the service obviously had been in full swing for an hour or more. The same total unconcern about the time element is exhibited in the Eastern services themselves. Not for the East the one-hour total which is all that modern westerners can endure. The service lasts two or three hours, and the worshippers last out the entire time on their feet instead of settling back in cushioned pews.

This superficial and to our minds incomprehensible difference between East and West is genuinely representative of a basic and much more important contrast. We of the West tend to act hastily, and we demand immediate results. Those failing us, we become discouraged; whereupon we either give up altogether, or search impatiently for new methods of procedure. The East, knowing that it is in touch with the everlasting, is little disposed to be upset or confused by the momentary. Through all the vicissitudes of history: through the furious theological debates which their own insistence upon definition produced; through the stormy career and the final collapse of the Eastern Empire of Byzantium; through the rise of the Muscovites and the inroads of the Turks; through the national revolutions of the Balkans and the economic revolution of Russia; through time and circumstance and beyond and above them, the Churches of the East have continued in their unruffled, unhurried, unfearing and uncompromising way.

Since we are not of the East, and since our own touch with Greek intellectual life is mediated through a variety of modifying and altering channels, few of us are of a mind or a mood to accept the Eastern ways for ourselves. Our spirit of enquiry has led us to doubt the possibility of knowing truth in final terms, and therefore has made us chary of precise formulation and definition. Our spirit of eagerness, which is characteristically Roman rather than Greek, has made us impatient of the relaxed and (to our minds) unproductive attitude of the Eastern ecclesiastics. Our concern for human values has made us extremely critical of the passivity of the Eastern Churches in the face of economic injustice and political oppression. For ourselves we are right on these points, and the East therefore is wrong—for us.

Yet it is worth asking whether even at these points we might learn from the East something of value for our so different world. The riddle of the universe remains unsolved. That does not excuse us from continuing the attempt to solve it. Disputes about values do often become disputes about the meaning of words. Yet we must use words, and we cannot jettison all problems of value. Time matters to us. But time matters because it is in the ongoing process of eternity, and so it is eternity after all that matters most.

It is noteworthy that the classic of Eastern Christianity, the Gospel from which our type sentences are drawn, defines eternal life precisely in qualitative rather than in quantitative terms. 'This is life eternal,' the Ephesian interpreter interjects into his account of Jesus' pastoral prayer; 'this is life eternal'—not that one shall live through all the centuries and beyond them, but that one shall 'know the only true God, and Jesus Christ whom he has sent.' Thus 'knowledge of the truth' categorically is equated with the 'life everlasting.' Thus the Eastern Christian heritage offers to us the final values of human experience bound together in the inseparable, indivisible value of the truth.

III

'OUTSIDE THE CHURCH THERE IS NO SALVATION'

(The Catholics)

'One Lord, one faith, one baptism.'—Ephesians 4:5 (AV).

'Outside the Church there is no salvation.'

—St. Cyprian, A.D. *c.* 250.

'WHY,' asked a very young student, 'do books on the Middle Ages say so much about Catholicism?' There are two answers. The obvious one is that Catholicism was the only form of Christianity existing in western Europe before the sixteenth century; and that accounts for the lack of mention of any other Christian pattern. The other reply, less commonly recognized but not less significant, is that Catholic Christianity was much more thoroughly determinative of life in general, before the Renaissance, than has been any form of Christianity anywhere since.

If we seek a descriptive rather than a merely chronological term to designate the period between the fall of Rome and the discovery of America, we scarcely shall find one more accurate than the word 'Christian.' The so-called 'Middle Ages' were the 'Christian age' *par excellence:* Christian in their intellectual assumptions, Christian in their moral valuations, Christian in their economic adjustments and in their political controls. There were in Europe, practically speaking, no non-Christians whatever. Far as many mediaeval Christians may have fallen below an absolute Christian ideal, none of them for a moment thought of disputing the ideal or of setting up an independent and contrasting scheme of values. And the Christianity which everyone took for granted was, of necessity, Catholic Christianity.

Since we stand, from the rise of Protestantism, less than one-fourth of the total chronological distance between Jesus of Nazareth and ourselves, we cannot but recognize that a chronological three-fourths of our own Christian heritage is expressly Catholic; and we may not suppose that fifteen centuries of continuous and organic growth failed to leave a very decided impress upon the thought and life of the four centuries which have followed. Our ways of thinking, our vocabulary, our symbols, our presuppositions, inevitably are colored by those which for so long were accepted unanimously by our forebears. In so far as we may claim to be Christian at all, we are driven in historical accuracy to own that in large degree we are Catholic.

We must remember, however, that just as the heritage of Protestantism is for fifteen hundred years Catholic, so also for a thousand years Catholicism was one with Orthodoxy. Thus both ancient Greek and ancient Latin Christianity persist in the Latin Christianity of today; and thus we who are Catholic are thereby and inescapably Orthodox also.

We have seen that the Greeks gave to Christianity its first intellectual formulation. Controversy over details of judgment led to the calling of the great Councils, which performed their function by writing and promulgating the great creeds of Christendom. The vocabulary of those creeds is that of Greek philosophy. The categories used are those of Greek dialectic. The concern of the creeds is preëminently the Greek concern for accuracy in discrimination and for precision in statement.

Those creeds came from Ecumenical Councils: that is, from assemblies representing the Church throughout the whole organized world of Europe and the Middle East. The creeds remained in the possession of Rome even when Rome separated herself from Constantinople; and they have remained in the possession of Protestants even though Protestantism declared itself independent of Rome. We are Catholic, therefore, first of all as to the theological pattern developed by the universal Church long before universality was confused by diversity.

Theology has been much deprecated and discounted in our time. A plea even for theological interest, let alone one for theological orthodoxy, meets immediate and almost automatic opposition from the average Protestant group. This modern coolness toward theological discussion commonly tries to defend itself by pointing to (a) the impossibility of arriving at absolute knowledge; and (b) the often tragic results of theological conflict. Actually, it may be suspected that our prevalent theological disinterest roots much more directly in ignorance and in sheer intellectual laziness. We have not been well taught in the theological realm, and we are reluctant to face the labor of learning in a new field now.

Of course we cannot have absolute knowledge. If we could, then indeed the study of theology would be meaningless. It is precisely the difficulty of learning, the impossibility of knowing, which makes the adventure of theological enquiry possible and significant. The Catholic Church soundly insists that no dogma shall be formulated until first it has been challenged: that is, until interest and investigation have reached a point so high that a consensus becomes possible. The creeds are not absolutes and finalities, and were not so understood by their makers. They are minimal declarations of what the conciliar majorities could agree upon; and they reflect the long and earnest and often incompletely resolved discussions of men who had done enough studying and thinking to be entitled to hold opinions.

Nor are we under compulsion to identify theological dogma with theological dictation. That sometimes feeling has run high in theological dispute but exhibits the importance which the disputants attached to their views. Such intellectual compulsion as has occurred in Christian history (and probably there has been less, proportionately, than late Protestant propaganda has led us to believe)—such intellectual compulsion as has occurred is involved in a tremendous complex of political interests and property concerns. That some have misused theology, to the disservice of mankind, is true but not very relevant. That theology may be used to man's service the Church always has contended, and they who are Catholic—they of any denomination who are Catholic—devoutly believe.

Is it a matter of indifference to us how the universe is organized and controlled? Is it outside our range of interest to identify the nature of moral values and the sources of moral judgment? Can it be irrelevant to human living to enquire into the destiny of human life? The real difference among men is not that some are theologians and some are not. The real difference is that some are interested in theology consciously and conscientiously, and so are good theologians; while others take their theology carelessly and unawarely, and so are bad theologians. The Catholic interest in theology is conscious and conscientious; and so when we are good theologians (that is, honest and intelligent and reverent theologians) we are Catholic.

A second and related Catholic essential is that which is specifically catholicism in lower case letters as well as with a capital: namely catholicity, universality. This universality exhibits itself in two principal ways. Seen from the standpoint of the living whole, it is the Catholic sense of community. Seen in terms of integrating structure, it is the Catholic principle of centrality. Catholicism is a fellowship, but a fellowship centrally and authoritatively guided. How has this centralized community functioned through the years? In what ways may we look still to its center, share in its fellowship?

A convenient symbol and a vital reality inhere in Catholicism's central act of worship: that of the sacrifice of the mass. Go where you will throughout the world, the service is the same. Come to any Catholic Church, on any Sunday or any Holy Day. We who know any other Catholic Church may take part immediately without a sense of strangeness. Decorations vary with local taste and usage. The announcements are made, and the sermon is preached, in a national tongue which may or may not be ours. The worshippers are dressed according to the contemporary custom of their own neighborhood. But the priest looks like the priest we know, the altar like our home altar; and at the Elevation of the Host we still may say, at one with all these fellows of ours whom we never have seen before, 'My Lord and my God!'

We have seen that the 'Middle Ages' were the Christian age. The Church was the single unifying factor in a Europe which otherwise was a pattern of self-sufficient and almost wholly separated neighborhoods. Local dialects moved toward their destiny as national languages; but among them all the churchly Latin served as the means of communication among men of whatsoever feudal allegiance. Held together by language and liturgy, Europe thereby came together in teaching and in judgment. Western Christendom was an integrated whole; and the integrating power of that Christian community was the centralized, Catholic, universal Church.

What was true of Catholicism in the Middle Ages remains visibly true of the Catholic community today. Rome is at the center, and so the Catholic knows whither he shall turn for guidance. Rome is at the center, and so Rome draws upon the thinking and living of all men everywhere for the intellectual and moral raw material which she distills in her unified and universal teaching. No empire has lasted so long, and certainly none has governed so completely. Conservator and disciplinarian, the Church has remained alive because she has focused the shifting forces of life and has channeled them through the courses of her age-old wisdom. Many have feared her, and some have hated; but few have presumed to ignore.

Another contemporarily disputed value, along with that of theological concern, is that of the Catholic insistence upon order. The Church began as a tiny fellowship, morally and intellectually at war with an overwhelmingly mighty pagan culture. It had to fight for its own survival, and with moral and intellectual weapons only. Early it learned that in order to fight effectively it must claim the fidelity of each member to the views and practices representing the consensus of all. St. Paul himself spoke of the Christian as a soldier, and of the Christian soldier's obligation not only to suffer hardship but also to obey orders.

The Catholic appreciation of order is evident in every manifestation of Catholic life. The hierarchy is fixed by tradition of many centuries' standing, and its members respect the rules and usages as a matter of course. The Catholic liturgy reflects the same basic attitude. Some Protestants have made it a matter of habit to attend Catholic rather than Protestant Sunday services, when visiting in a strange town, for the reason that in any event the sermon may reasonably be expected to be dull, but that in the case of the Catholic Church one may count at least on a significant ritual dignifiedly and reverently conducted.

Nor is the Catholic sermon always and necessarily dull. Abilities of preachers within any given religious community vary as greatly as do abilities of carpenters or machinists. The Catholic genius for order is highly apparent when one hears Dominican clerics expounding the theology of their leader and hero, St. Thomas Aquinas. Often the premises of the argument will not satisfy the non-Catholic. But the premises once granted, the reasoning moves surely, accurately, cogently, to its inevitable logical outcome. Attendance at Dominican services well might be made a requirement for Protestant students of homiletics who need to be cured of the intellectual fuzziness and inexcusable illogic so pitifully evident in many Protestant expositions of a fuzzy and illogical faith.

In the course of subsequent enquiries into Protestantism and liberalism we shall notice, and it is to be hoped that we shall appreciate fully, the usefulness of independence and dissent. Ere we do that, we shall be profited by observing the worth of coherence and conformity. A fellowship exists only by agreement, and agreement only by the subordinating of individual predilections to the common will. An army is an army only as its constituent battalions, and their constituent soldiers, follow a course centrally determined and centrally directed. The Church is at once an army and a fellowship: a fellowship as to its inner relations, an army as to its outer. To be either (and to be a living Church it must be both) it must accept and enforce discipline among its members.

This Catholicism discerned at the outset, this it has believed and practised through the centuries. As a Church it has been therefore effective and long-lived. As an army it has been successful, as a fellowship it has been rich in meaning. Most of those who will read this book are not Catholic organizationally, and never will be. Unless we choose to become Catholic morally, in this area of discipline within the fellowship, we may look forward to nothing but complete social and personal disintegration.

Clear thinking; genuine fellowship; constructive order: by these means historic Catholicism has attained these also as ends. Human weakness indeed has confused the issues by argument, has violated the fellowship in selfishness, has misused the discipline in harshness. That was to be expected, and is to be expected in any association of fallible men and women. Human weakness has been transmuted into strength, nevertheless, as debate found its way to decision; as the motley mass of humankind has found an acceptable and accepted ground of oneness; as discipline has expressed itself in that order which is necessary to constructive, coherent, continuing life.

Intellectually many of us cannot be Roman Catholic, because we resist those implications of centrality and order which demand that the individual shall surrender his judgment at all crucial points to the final dictum of the Church. We need the Church as guide and counsellor, but we are not willing to accept it as dictator for ourselves, and we are not willing that it shall dictate to anyone else. Thus we could not accept Catholic confirmation without mental reservations; and we could not live as Catholics without having sooner or later to choose between open rebellion and flat intellectual dishonesty.

Nevertheless we remain Catholic, all of us, in the proud heritage which western Europe has given us: a heritage which wars and contentions have blurred but shall not quite destroy. We are Catholic in the permanent framework of our thought and in much of its persisting content. We are Catholic in our vision of one humanwide, human-deep community of likeminded persons. We are Catholic in readiness to be integral parts of an organic society. We are Catholic, then, in so far as we accept our place within the Catholic, universal fellowship of men.

Outside the structure of the Roman Catholic Church, despite the word of St. Cyprian, we believe that we can find salvation. Outside the Church of vigorous thinking, of cordial association, of willing self-control, there can be no salvation for any of us. Without appreciation of that particular organized body which first gave us these values, there can be no reasonable understanding of what we ourselves are. On these rocks which have withstood the hammering of the centuries: these rocks of teaching and community and order: the Church is founded; and every Church, and every fellowship, which rightly may claim the right to live.

IV

'I CAN NO OTHER'

(The Lutherans)

'*The just shall live by faith.*'—Habakkuk 2:4 (AV); quoted by St. Paul in Galatians 3:11 and in Romans 1:17.

'*The good man lives in his fidelity.*'—Habakkuk 2:4 (GH).

'*Here I stand. I can no other. God help me. Amen.*'—(Traditional) words of Martin Luther before the Diet of Worms, A.D. 1521.

THERE are some eighty millions of Lutherans in the world. Only about two and a half millions of them are in the United States. Yet all who accept the Protestant heritage, who accept it in any way and to any extent, are Lutheran too. We shall profit therefore by exploring the values for which Lutheranism has stood these more than four hundred years, values which all of us share and should try more fully to understand. Thanking the Lutherans for what they have given us, we shall thank them the more when we know more clearly what it is.

Martin Luther was born of German peasant stock in 1483, nine years before Columbus landed in America. This man who was to discover a new world of religious experience and life began by belonging thoroughly to the world that then was. He took bachelor's and master's degrees at the University of Erfurt; and in 1505, when he was twenty-two years old, he became an Augustinian monk.

Three years later he was appointed Professor of Philosophy in the newly established University of Wittenberg. As a scholar he began to think his way toward a new interpretation of Christianity in terms of personal faith. As a Churchman he saw, and increasingly was distressed by, much that seemed to him to be superstition and dishonesty approved in high places. Thought and observation joined to drive him into protest; and in 1517 he challenged the official Church position on the question of what were called 'indulgences.'

That question now has become badly confused in our minds, and not least because of the subsequent development of Protestant propaganda. In fairness to the Roman Church we must recognize that 'indulgences' were not permissions to commit sin, and that they never were officially declared to save anyone from the sufferings of Purgatory. They were simply clearances from earthly punishment for sins already committed; and they were given (in theory, at least) only to those who had done enough good to balance their deeds of evil.

The real difficulty began to arise when giving money for the building of St. Peter's Church in Rome came to be regarded as being in itself a good work meriting 'indulgence.' Inevitably this financial sort of 'good work' became practically a cash buying of forgiveness; and through the intellectual and moral confusions of both clergy and laity, the whole affair turned into a commercial deal between the Church and the sinner. It was only natural, too, that some people should think of transferring their merit, thus secured by purchase, to loved ones who had died without clearing their own records; and thus the notion of escape from Purgatory became involved in the whole 'indulgence' situation.

It was against confusions and abuses of these kinds that Martin Luther protested. Having challenged the Church, he was accused of heresy. Defending his position as to details, and being promptly overruled, he was driven to deny the authority of the Church and so of the Pope. In 1520 Luther was excommunicated, and the break became absolute. The Elector Frederick of Saxony, who had his own political reasons for wanting to break Roman power in Northern Europe, protected Luther from any punishment more physical. Other German princes aligned themselves with Frederick, and so found themselves supporters of Luther. From 1523 until his death in 1546, Luther was the religious leader of Northern Germany and the political ally of its rulers. Thus Lutheranism was born, and Protestantism in it.

Northern continental Europe became and remained Lutheran. The Lutheran Churches were established as the state Churches of North Germany and Scandinavia. Immigrants to the United States from these regions brought their faith with them, and soon set up their own Lutheran Churches to express it. Probably the first stable Lutheran community on this continent was that of the Swedes who colonized the mouth of the Delaware in 1638; which means that the Lutheran Churches have been part of our national religious life for now more than three centuries. Until recently a majority of American Lutheran Churches held at least some of their services in the languages of their respective mother countries. They tend still to cling very closely to their old traditions; and so their contribution is authentically that of the movement from which they sprang, the movement which bore Luther's name.

What centrally did Martin Luther have to say? What has Lutheranism given to the world that is worth having and keeping? It is important to remember that Luther did not start out to create a new Church. He was interested only in glorifying the old one. The special emphases of the Lutheran movement grow, all of them, out of the developing dispute between Luther and the Church authorities. All of them are inter-related, depending each upon each other, and all upon the special circumstances of Luther's career. As we try now to look at them separately, we must remember that they belong together and cannot be separated in historic fact.

Since the story of Luther is the story of an argument, of a series of arguments, its details belong in a framework of debate. In two principal (though overlapping) areas, Luther condemned what the Church was doing and came therefore to deny what it was saying. One of these areas was that of the way of salvation. Was a Christian to be saved by his works, as the Church taught, or by his faith, as Luther had come to believe? Once that dispute had arisen, and in it the Church had declared Luther to be wrong, the issue turned necessarily to the underlying question of authority. Was truth (here or in any realm) determined by the Church, or was it to be measured by some other standard? These two questions, and the development of the Lutheran answers to them, concern all of us all the time, because for all of us they are questions that need ever to be answered.

Reading St. Paul in the quiet of his study, the young Professor Luther noticed that 'faith' seemed to be the keynote of the apostle's teaching; and in the letters to the Galatians and to the Romans he found flat denials of the view that salvation could be gained by 'works.' Meanwhile, in the life of the Church about him, Luther not only saw salvation offered for 'works,' but also noted that 'works' themselves were understood in a very formal and sometimes indeed (as we have seen) in a purely financial sense. Angered by the abuses which he observed, strengthened inwardly by his reading of St. Paul, Luther took his first steps toward the break with Rome.

The more he argued, the more sharply he insisted upon the differences. Since 'faith' was at least as difficult to define as it was to achieve, it came to be pretty narrowly interpreted as a matter of intellectual opinion. Since in order to repudiate the 'work' of buying indulgences Luther had found himself denying the validity of the theory of 'good works' altogether, he slipped rather easily into discounting matters of conduct and discipline. Lutheranism began as a protest, and went on to become a division. It is not surprising that through the years the Protestants have kept on protesting and dividing.

Luther himself never was so limited in his view of the relative importance of faith and works as many of his lesser followers have been. In Luther's own life 'faith' certainly was much more than mere theological opinion. It was absolute confidence in the power and the grace of God. It was warm conviction of the right as he saw the right. It was the kind of fidelity which made possible Luther's courage against all the world: 'Here I stand. I can no other.'

Nor is it proper to suppose that Luther was wholly indifferent to Christian conduct. He was not. He insisted on honesty, and morality, and good will. It is true, however, that he inclined to restrict the applying of moral standards to the individual's immediate behavior apart from social and political considerations. Largely because he had seen the ill effects of Churchly dominance over the state, Luther swung to an extreme in which, in substance, he freed the state not only from Churchly dictation but also from moral judgment. But his central emphasis as to Christian conduct was one we can understand, one all of us can accept. It was simply that Christian behavior was not something one chose for the sake of reward, but rather something one inevitably carried out through the inner impulsion of Christian experience.

This leads us to notice one very important contribution which Lutheranism has made to religious life, in the matter of what the Christian service of worship is designed to do. The Lutheran service is by no means devoid of ritual, by no means denies all the old forms. But there are striking differences between its usages and others that we know. The minister does less than does the Catholic priest, except that for purposes of teaching and argument he commonly preaches much longer. The congregation, on the other hand, does rather more than do the Catholic laity; and, what is more significant, does different things and in a different way.

The Catholic theory of worship is basically one of works. It is that by worship we do something to please God, and so to gain his favor for ourselves. The Lutheran theory of worship is specifically one of faith. It is that in worship we accept the grace of God, which ever is available to those who will receive it as God's free gift in Christ.

Sitting to sing the hymns, and singing them in rather quiet and leisurely fashion, are exact symbols of the Lutheran view. The Lutheran does not expect to do something for God. He rather waits for God to do something for him; and his faith therefore is expressed not so much in action as in receptivity.

Theologically and practically, Lutheranism has suffered: or so it will seem to some of us: by interpreting the distinction between 'faith' and 'works' much more narrowly than St. Paul and Luther ever intended it. Starting by deprecating those 'works' which were purely formal observance, Lutheranism has been inclined to discount the realm of conduct altogether. Eagerly accepting inward faith as the touchstone of life, the Lutheran people too often have limited Christian 'faith' to the accepting of Luther's own sixteenth-century opinions. Thus in trying to escape a formalism of action, Lutheranism not seldom has become entangled in a new formalism of ideas.

At this point we come inevitably to the second major issue in the continuing dispute between Lutheran and Catholic, as it was the second phase of the debate between Luther himself and the Bishops of his time. It is the question as to the seat of authority. Defied by Luther as to its practices, the Church replied by asserting that it could not be challenged because it was infallibly right in all that it chose formally to declare. Still rejecting the practices which thus had been confirmed, Luther could find no way out but to reject also the authority which had confirmed them. 'Then,' argued the defenders of the Churchly tradition, 'what authority do you propose to substitute for that of the Church?'

Most of us today would be willing to reply, 'We are content with the authority of the individual conscience.' Luther in fact did stand on just this ground. But intellectually his age was not ready to state it in such terms, nor was he. He had to find something external which would authenticate his position; and readily enough he found it in the Bible. The Bible said nothing about indulgences, and for a time Luther thought it said nothing about Purgatory. Then, when a Catholic disputant pointed out the implication of Purgatory in the Second Book of Maccabees, the Lutherans were forced into the further step of throwing that book out of the Bible: and with it, by the necessity of formal categories, all the associated works of the Greek canon which we call the Apocrypha.

Actually Luther was pretty free in his handling of the Bible. He disliked the book of Esther, which he said contained 'a superfluity of heathen naughtiness.' He dismissed the letter of James, which argued mightily for works as against faith, as 'a letter of straw' (recht ströherne). And when in the work of translating the Bible into German he came to the obscure and difficult book of Revelation, he concluded that it was so likely to do more harm than good that he put it into the appendix along with the discarded Apocrypha.

But formally Luther did insist that the Bible was the complete and infallible Word of God. He translated it into German; and while sometimes he despaired of doing the job adequately (it is said that once he threw down his pen, crying, 'Ach, Gott! it is so hard to make these Hebrew prophets speak German!'), his achievement not only gave the Scriptures to his people in their own language, but also stabilized for them a language which ever since has maintained the same essential forms.

Luther's followers, being lesser men than he, paid more attention to his formal, general statements than they did to his personal practice; and so they have been much more insistent than was he on the literal infallibility of the Biblical text. Protestant devotion to the Bible, and, alas!, much of Protestant quibbling about the meaning of the Bible, stem directly from this substitution of the authority of a Book for that of a Church.

The denial of Churchly authority meant also, as we have seen, an emphasizing of the power of the secular political state. Luther on principle opposed Church dictation in political affairs. Beyond that, circumstances led him to accept the support of German princes who were seeking their independence from the Church, and so circumstances tempted him into approving almost everything that those princes did. The blackest mark in Luther's record unquestionably is that of his opposition to the Peasants' Revolt in 1524 and 1525: he advised the princes 'to burn, to slay, to destroy' these humble and devoutly religious people who were contending for a freer and more abundant life for themselves.

What came out of this liberation of the state from ecclesiastical controls thus was not a real separation of Church and state, but rather the subordinating of the Church to the state. This attitude has been maintained by most Lutheran groups ever since. As a consequence the Lutheran clergy usually have insisted on their complete neutrality in all political matters, and have been reluctant to admit any moral implications in political issues. This is why so large a part of German Protestantism failed to make any effective protest against the rise of Nazi tyranny. This too is why Lutheran Churches in the United States have been relatively slow to engage in any discussion of public affairs.

The greatest contribution of the Lutheran movement to religious life was not quite an explicit one, and was mentioned only indirectly during the controversies we have noticed. But it was there in Luther, it was there in his followers, it persists today as a direct heritage from him who dared to stand alone and unshaken before his enemies at the Diet of Worms. It is that of the absolute right of the individual to be absolutely himself. 'Here *I* stand,' cries Luther, '*I* can no other.'

This individual emphasis does appear, in theological terms, in the Lutheran insistence on 'the priesthood of all believers.' The point of view was developed, of course, as an attack upon the claim of the priests of the Church to dictate to the people in all matters of faith and conscience. In contrast Lutheranism asserted every man's right to approach God on his own account, and therefore to understand God's will within his own judgment. Far more than it was stated, and in spite of its partial negation in Lutheran emphasis upon the authority of the Bible, individualism was practised by Luther and by those who followed him. Catholicism was and remained essentially a community, subordinating the person to the group and to the institution. Protestantism began as an individual protest. It became a movement of individuals, of individuality, and so of individualism.

Some of us may think (as the writer personally does) that the Protestants went much too far in that direction;

and we may observe with satisfaction that modern Protestant Christianity (the Lutheran, however, still largely ex-
cepted) is turning again to communal realization and to
communal action. Nevertheless we cannot but be grateful
for the simple heroism of the one man who dares to stand
alone against the opinion of his time, the authorities of his
time, the powers of his time; the man who dares to stand
alone just because he is convinced that he is right.

All of us who are Protestant are Lutheran, then, in the
positive terms of the Lutheran movement. We account the
inward attitude of the individual, the faith in values which
makes him faithful to them, to be the touchstone of religious living. We may know the Bible, may seek to learn
from it, as few laymen had any chance to do before Luther
put it within the people's reach. We honor the courage of
all those who have stood for their own faith, for the authority of their own conscience, against whatever opposition might arise. These are Lutheranism's gifts to us all.

Within the Lutheran Churches today there are signs that
the less happy consequences of Luther's personal history
are being challenged and to some extent set aside. Christian
conduct is being seen more largely as concerned with all
the aspects of human living. Disputes about the literal
meaning of the Bible are giving way to concern for vitally
significant truth discovered in human experience. 'Faith'
thus is conceived as opinion less than it used to be, and
'works' are not denied so totally as once they were.

Thus the Lutheran division of the Protestant army, the
first to be activated and the first to fight, now is being
aided, and its character is being somewhat modified, by the
new divisions which have come to join it. The gradual

dropping of European languages from Lutheran services in the United States reflects the naturalizing of Lutheranism into the general American pattern. We may expect the Lutheran Churches of the future to be a little less rigid in their ideas, a good deal broader in their interests.

Let us hope, however, that they never will become so flexible as to be spineless, so broad as to be shallow. Their sturdy independence, their loyalty to their tradition, their demand for faith and for faithfulness, they offer us as their continuing gifts. Thanks to them and with them we may be independent too, and loyal, and faithful. The good man lives in his fidelity. When we have found what for us is the truth, there let us stand. God helping us, we can no other.

V

'TO GLORIFY GOD'

(The Presbyterians)

'I am the Lord, and there is none else. I form the light, and create darkness: I make peace, and create evil: I the Lord do all these things.'—Isaiah 45:7 (AV).

'All things work together for good to them that love God, to them who are the called according to his purpose.'
—Romans 8:28 (AV).

Q. 'What is the chief end of man?' A. 'To glorify God, and enjoy him for ever.'
—Westminster Shorter Catechism, A.D. 1647.

BEHIND the dikes and along the canals of Holland; in little boats crossing the English Channel in the dark of night; on the craggy hillsides and deep in the glens of Scotland; in the strange new setting of Northern Ireland; in a yet stranger and newer land across the Western Ocean; through the passes of the Alleghenies and far over the plains and the prairies: here lived and hither journeyed, here believed and onward hoped, those Christians who followed the lead of John Calvin, the members of the Reformed branch of Protestantism which most commonly we call 'Presbyterian.' There are only about eight millions of them in the world, and almost half of those are in the

39

United States. They have had an influence upon mankind far beyond what might have been expected of their numbers.

Late in the year 1533 or early in 1534 a young French lawyer, having heard much of the religious ferment in Northern Europe and having experienced much of religious ferment in his own heart, chose for himself to follow the lead of Luther in breaking from the traditional Church. That, at least, is the way we would put it, looking at his decision from outside. It is important to notice that he himself described it otherwise. He called it his conversion to Christian faith. Jean Cauvin, whom we know as John Calvin, always respected and admired Luther; but he thought for himself, he acted on his own responsibility, and so he made his own distinctive contribution to the religious life of the western world.

Forced in 1536 to flee from his native France, Calvin thought to stop overnight in Geneva, in Switzerland. A friend of his there, one Guillaume Farel, a year before had persuaded the city's government to declare the community Protestant by edict. Farel urged Calvin to stay and to serve the Protestant movement through the local Churches. After much argument, and reluctantly, Calvin consented. Very soon the Protestant Churches of Geneva, recognized and approved by the authorities, took over effective control of the procedure of the government itself; and Calvin, as the most able and most vigorous of the Church leaders, became the actual civil ruler.

Again, however, we must observe that Calvin phrased it in another way. The form of government which he instituted and operated was, to his mind, not an *auto*cracy: rule by himself; but very positively a *theo*cracy: rule by

God. How might one learn the will of God as ruler of the people? The lawyer found an answer ready-made, in the 'law of Moses,' the legal sections of the Old Testament. Lawyer John Calvin proceeded to interpret this ancient code to suit the conditions of the time; and this body of interpretations became the authoritative standard in all the aspects of Geneva's life.

Two years' strenuous enforcement of so rigorous a system proved to be all the citizens were willing then to take; and in 1538 Calvin was forced out of authority and out of town. For three years he taught and preached in Strassbourg, in Lorraine. Here he met, talked with, and influenced Protestant refugees from many European regions, and so greatly hastened the spreading of his ideas. Geneva meanwhile fell into confusion, and by majority wish of her citizens brought Calvin back to straighten things out. His God-centered government continued to be vigorous and stringent; but it was high-principled and efficient, and as to both education and economics it brought Geneva well to the fore among the cities of Europe.

From Calvin and Geneva the stream flowed into the French Huguenot movement, into the national Church of the Netherlands, through John Knox into the life of the people of Scotland. The stream was one commingled of theology and of practice: of a theology and a practice very clear and very logical, very orderly and very closely related each to the other. The stream still flows, and has entered into many channels not marked with its particular name. At the same time it too has been modified from other sources. This Calvinistic stream in the world's life, and its influence on the world, and its being influenced by the world, we try now to see, to measure, and to understand.

Calvinism dominated for a time even the religious life of England. During the Puritan ascendancy in the mid-seventeenth century the authoritative statements of the Reformed faith, as held by its British adherents, were set forth officially at London in the 'Westminster Confession' and in the 'Longer' and 'Shorter' Catechisms. The single question from the 'Shorter Catechism' which stands at the head of this chapter indicates the first essential of the Calvinistic view at once of the universe and of human life. 'What is the chief end of man?' 'To glorify God, and enjoy him for ever.' God is the beginning of all things, and he is no less their goal and their end. The first requisite for man, then, can be no other than humility before God.

To insist on the absolute power of God inevitably is to take a definite position about the freedom of man: inevitably is to regard man's freedom as sharply limited by the divine purpose. The two systems of religious thought which most urgently stress God's authority in the universe, Calvinism and the Arabian faith of Islam, agree necessarily in regarding man's personal destiny as fixed by divine command. The first consequence of this position is to make man feel very small and weak indeed *vis-à-vis* the Almighty; and this both Calvin and Muhammad do as to their followers. A second result, following just as closely, is the insistence that man's first and everlasting obligation is implicitly to accept and to obey the divine will: this no less both Presbyterianism and Islam have taught.

In such a way of thinking, the glorifying of God necessarily is the chief end of man. No other Christian tradition has concerned itself so much with God as has the Calvinistic. No other has made such stringent demands for man's obedience. The converse of the absolute power and absolute rightness of God of course had to be the absolute wrongness of man. The theological expression of this was the doctrine called 'total depravity.' The point of the orthodox Calvinist is that all men are by nature evil; and so that no one at all deserves to be saved, no one has any personal claim upon the divine grace. What we all do have, the only thing we have, is the simple obligation to obey God. What some of us may obtain is God's favor, freely given. For this we may, we must, be thankful. But as we have no way of knowing on whom the favor will fall, we have no ground for self-satisfaction either as to what we may do or as to what God may do for us.

The important moral aspect of this attitude is sharply pointed by the Satan's sardonic question in the book of Job, 'Doth Job serve God for naught?' The Calvinistic answer is simply, 'Yes, of course he serves God for naught; and he should, and so should every man.' To serve God for rewards, or to escape punishments, is small and cheap and unworthy. To serve God because one ought to serve him, and that regardless of what God may do with his servant, is the only adequate kind of service. 'Though he slay me, yet will I trust him,' cries Job; and the good Calvinist accepts life or death with equal mind, never claiming that what little he has done, or can do, merits the slightest consideration in the determining of his personal fate.

There are of course some intellectual difficulties about this kind of determinism, and some practical ones too. The emphasis upon God's absolute and unlimited power scarcely can be maintained without raising some embarrassing questions about God's ethical character. Calvin was able to accept without hesitancy such a view as that stated by the second Isaiah, 'I am the Lord . . . I make peace, and create evil.' Some of us will be unhappy about that, will doubt and challenge it. Yet hitherto we have found no more logical solution of the problem of evil than that which the Calvinist propounds. And we must remember that the Calvinist, holding that all that happens expresses God's will, therefore sees all that happens as being by definition ultimately good.

Again, if human destiny be thought of as settled by God's will alone, apart from anything a man may or may not do, the issue arises as to whether man does anything whatever by his own will; and if not, whether there is any meaning at all in man's moral effort. To this puzzling query Calvinism answers clearly, if not to all of us convincingly, that moral effort is part of the divine requirement of us, and that we must make it anyway. It is not surprising that some other Protestant groups, notably the Methodist, have reacted sharply from this attitude and have stressed instead the part played by a man's own free choice in shaping his life and that of the world. At the same time it is evident that through four centuries Calvinistic faith in the divine command has brought a rich harvest of courageous and faithful living.

The whole position is summed up in the hymn written by Norman McLeod, Moderator of the Church of Scotland in the mid-nineteenth century, which begins, 'Courage, brother, do not stumble,' and whose reiterated refrain is, 'Trust in God, and do the right.' Trust in God, because there is nothing else one can do. Do the right, because that is what God demands. This, says the witness of Calvinism, is the whole duty of man.

Faithful living thus follows inescapably from devout humility. Or, since the center and source of life is seen by the Calvinist as existing not in man but in God, the second major element of Presbyterian tradition perhaps should be identified rather as that of discipline. It was by discipline, by the rule of the Old Testament law, that the lawyer Calvin directed the life of Geneva. It has been by discipline that Dutch parents have brought up their children, by discipline that Scottish and Scotch-Irish sturdiness has made its impact on the western world. It is by discipline that the Presbyterian Churches yet maintain their strength and perform their chosen mission.

The structure of Presbyterian Church government is indicated in the name. The 'presbyter' is the Greek *presbyteros*, which means simply the 'elder,' the senior. Calvin found in the New Testament abundant evidence that the early Christian communities, following the example of the Jewish Synagogue, had looked for guidance and control to the older members of their several groups. In Geneva he developed this pattern of government by 'elders' in contrast to the monarchical rule of Bishops on the one hand, to the anarchy of undirected impulse on the other.

The affairs of each local Presbyterian Church today are controlled by a group of 'elders,' 'presbyters,' chosen from and by the congregation. The minister is technically the 'teaching elder,' while the leading laymen are the 'ruling elders.' Beyond the local Church the structure is one of a series of courts: in ascending order the Presbytery (a relatively small district, such as a single metropolitan area); the Synod (a larger region, not uncommonly a single State); and the General Assembly (the final authority for the Church within the nation).

What issues in practice from this type of structure may be described as a disciplined democracy. It is genuinely a democracy, for the people make their own selection of their leaders. It is effectively disciplined, for the selected leaders have authority and use it. The consequence is that Presbyterianism as a whole moves slowly and with caution, but that nevertheless it does move. Conservative because it depends heavily both upon its ancient tradition and upon the judgments of its older members now living, it is also progressive in that the Church reacts in the long run to the changing attitudes of its entire membership.

One particular aspect of personal and group discipline has been so much stressed by the Presbyterians, from Calvin's time onward, that it must be mentioned as a third great characteristic of the movement as a whole. This is the discipline of the intellect, the demand for trained intelligence. Calvin could build his majestic structure of theological teaching, could promulgate and defend it, because he had a great mind: a mind great not only in its native endowment, but great also through the rigorous training he had received in the law. He insisted that no one was worthy to lead, whether in theological thinking or in practical administration, who lacked intelligence or who lacked the training to make his intelligence useful.

Through all the years the Presbyterians have been foremost among the Protestant denominations in insisting upon the highest possible standards for admission to the ministry. Candidates are required to show that they have capacity for real study and thinking; and then, through the colleges and the theological schools, they are required to study and to think. (Characteristically and significantly, the Presbyterian seminaries yet are resisting the general trend toward the abandonment of required study of Hebrew and Greek.)

This concern for an educated ministry, shared ever by the Presbyterian laymen, has made the laymen educated too. Nowhere else in Protestantism has the sermon played so crucial a part in the life of the Church, and nowhere else has it faced so much of healthy criticism from the pews. The 'sermon-taster' is a notable figure of Scottish Church life: the layman (or lay woman) who watches for every slightest flaw of structure or of doctrine, who rejoices in a point cogently made, who criticizes without mercy and yet without malice.

One outcome of this intellectual interest has been that controversy within Reformed circles is most likely to turn upon intellectual matters, and so principally on points of Christian doctrine. Episcopalians argue among themselves on questions of ritual usage, such as genuflections or the vestments to be worn on particular occasions. Methodists are likely to quarrel over issues of Christian behavior, whether dancing or playing cards (as in the last century) or bearing arms in war (as today). It is in the Presbyterian Churches that theology really is a matter of active interest to everyone; and so it is among the Presbyterians that theological disputes receive the most attention.

This is why 'Fundamentalism,' as a self-conscious and specifically titled movement, began a quarter-century ago in a Presbyterian Church in Los Angeles. This is why Westminster Theological Seminary even more recently was set up as a protest against what were considered the 'heresies' now being taught at Princeton. This is why, in many cities, one will find two major Presbyterian

Churches, one of them extremely conservative and the other confessedly liberal. The point is that Presbyterians are accustomed to think about their faith, and to think that their thinking matters.

Inevitably the years have modified many of the sharp lines of the original Calvinist pattern. With glorious inconsistency: glorious, because its motive and its outcome alike are noble: the Presbyterian of today calls on men and women to accept for themselves the grace of God which in theory God gives or withholds regardless of what man may do. With human optimism that contravenes a gloomy theology, the Presbyterian of today effectively denies the total depravity of man in his confidence that man can and will find and do the will of God. With the resilience of a disciplined freedom the Presbyterian of today moves into ever new patterns of social adjustment and organization.

But he has not abandoned his heritage wholly; and, what matters more, all of us have gained that heritage in part. We have learned from the Presbyterian, and are learning, that the adventure of life rests upon faith because there is nothing else it can rest on. We have learned, and are learning, that discipline of our spirits is requisite not for the gaining of personal advantage but for the avoidance of personal and social chaos. We have learned, and are learning, that he who refuses to study and to think has no right to express an opinion, whether about religion or in any other field.

To sloppy sentimentality, which so easily attaches itself to religious eagerness, the Presbyterians offer a necessary and a vital corrective. It may be that they need to hear from some of the rest of us more about the love of God. No less do we need to hear from them more about the will of God. They have been rigid, and to some extent will be; and by being rigid, they will help to save others of us from being wishy-washy. Their theory about man starts in pessimism, by declaring his total evilness. It issues in the highest optimism, in its positive assertion of man's duty to do his duty. 'Trust in God, and do the right.' This is the chief end of man: and this is the final glorifying of God.

VI

'THE WHOLE STATE OF CHRIST'S CHURCH'

(The Episcopalians)

'*Honour all men. Love the brotherhood. Fear God. Honour the king.*'—I Peter 2:17 (AV).

'*Endeavouring to keep the unity of the Spirit in the bond of peace.*'—Ephesians 4:3 (AV).

'*Then shall the Priest say, Let us pray for the whole state of Christ's Church.*'—The Order for the Holy Communion, *First Prayer Book of Edward VI*, A.D. 1549; restored to this simple form in *The Book of Common Prayer* (Protestant Episcopal), A.D. 1929.

'*Be of good comfort, Master Ridley, we shall this day light such a candle, by God's grace, in England, as I trust shall never be put out.*'—Last words of Hugh Latimer, Bishop of Worcester, to Bishop Ridley of London, before their execution, 16 October 1555.

How old is the Church of England? It is clear that Christianity reached the island of Britain not later than the second century of our era; and some very old traditions identify the first missionary as Joseph of Arimathea, that citizen of Jerusalem who had provided the tomb for the burial of Jesus. When Rome fell, the pagan Saxons invaded the distant island and seized all its kindlier and more fertile regions. The Christian Church, driven with its Celtic members into the mountain recesses of Wales and Scotland and across the water to Ireland, began in time to send missionaries back into those regions where some Celtic population remained; but it made no serious attempt to reach the Saxons now settled in the southern half of Britain.

There is a familiar and charming tradition to the effect that Pope Gregory I, seeing some fair-haired lads offered for sale in the slave-market in Rome, and learning that they were 'Angles,' commented that they should be called, and ought to become, 'angels': *'non Angli sed angeli.'* Whether or not this started St. Gregory to thinking about a mission to Angle-land, it is sure that in the year 597 he sent his friend and colleague Augustine (not, of course, the North African author of the *Confessions* and of *The City of God*) as the leader of a missionary party. This second St. Augustine was lucky enough to find a French Christian Queen in a southeastern Saxon kingdom; and with her aid he succeeded in persuading the King himself to conversion. Thus occurred a second founding of the Church of England; and St. Augustine himself became the first Archbishop of Canterbury.

The English Church remained Roman for more than nine hundred years, despite acute conflicts with the Papacy in the reigns of Henry II and of John, until the Reformation on the Continent was well under weigh. In 1521 none other than Henry VIII wrote an attack upon Lutheranism for which he received from the Pope the title of 'Defender of the Faith': a title which he chose to keep after the break from Rome, and which has been proudly borne by all his successors on the English throne. In 1527 Tyndale's English New Testament, printed secretly at Cologne and regarded as Protestant and heretical, was solemnly burned

in public under the authority of the English Archbishop
Warham.

Then arose the notorious quarrel over Henry's divorce
from Catherine of Aragon. Negotiations dragged through
years, ending with a complete break and Henry's excom-
munication by the Pope in March of 1534. The new national spirit, which was rising everywhere in western Europe, found in this episode means to express itself in
England. In June, 1534, the English Bishops decided, with
only one voting in the negative, that the Bishop of Rome
had no jurisdiction over them. In November of the same
year Parliament passed the Act of Supremacy, declaring
the King to be 'the supreme head of the Church of England.' Thus the Church may be said to have been founded
for a third time.

When the English came to this continent they brought
their Church with them. Probably the first Church of England service held on this side of the Atlantic was that conducted by the Reverend Francis Fletcher, chaplain to the
expedition of Sir Francis Drake, just north of San Francisco Bay in the summer of 1579. While Puritans and Independents settled New England, and the Quakers Pennsylvania, Virginia was Anglican from the outset, as were
Georgia and the Carolinas, and as New York became when
the English displaced the Dutch.

The Bishops in the American colonies, being appointees
and official agents of the British Crown, inevitably were
Tories in the days of the Revolution, and so they had to
flee the country. It was not until 1784 that new Bishops
for America were consecrated, and then it was by Bishops
of the Scottish Episcopal Church. Afterwards English

Bishops joined also in consecration; and the two lines of succession were united in 1792 in what was named 'The Protestant Episcopal Church in the United States of America.' It was called 'Protestant,' of course, to mark its difference from Roman Catholicism; and 'Episcopal' because it accepted the leadership of Bishops in contrast to the government by elders in Presbyterian usage, to congregational independence in the Churches of New England.

The Protestant Episcopal Church now has almost two million members. How many people belong to the parent Church of England, or to the affiliated bodies in the British Dominions, it is difficult to say, since all Englishmen are regarded as being within the national religious fellowship unless they declare otherwise. As we think of the Episcopalians, we concern ourselves both with the Church of England and with the Protestant Episcopal Church in our own country. These Churches are one in tradition, one in essential character, one in type of organization, one in customs of worship, one in their feeling of kinship each to the other. What are they like?

A distinguished American theologian once defined the Episcopal Church as 'a body of men and women bound together by a Prayer Book, who agree to differ on all questions of any possible importance.' Many non-Episcopalians, observing Episcopal usage, are impressed by what seems to them to be an extreme ceremonialism. A young Methodist fresh from one of the Dakotas said to the writer, after his first attendance at a service in Trinity Church, Boston, 'Maybe the Lord knows their downsittings and their uprisings, but I certainly didn't.' And there is the judgment reflected in the gay and familiar story of the stately Church whose head usher described it as being 'no place to get religion.'

Such remarks of course are flippant in themselves; but each of them does represent something recognizable in the Episcopal way of doing things. Agreement to disagree; ceremonial; emotional restraint: these seem to characterize the Anglican tradition. We shall want then to ask two questions about them: first, how did these qualities begin and develop? second, are they faults in the Episcopal Church, or can they reasonably be defended?

The answers to both questions are available in the recognition of what this Church is. It is two things predominantly: it is English, and it is Catholic. On these two relationships hang all its attitude and all its practice.

The Church of England is English in continuing fact. The Protestant Episcopal Church in America is English in heritage and very largely so in sentiment. An element of primary significance is the use of the English language in the services. 'It is a thing plainly repugnant to the Word of God,' declares the XXIVth Article of Religion, 'and the custom of the Primitive Church, to have publick Prayer in the Church, or to minister the Sacraments, in a tongue not understanded of the people.' Thus in its declaration of independence from Rome the Church brought its message directly to the minds of the English common folk; and the impact of comprehensible words, suddenly available after many years of services not understood at all, must have been mighty indeed.

This happened, we should remember, at just the time when Spenser and Marlowe and Shakespeare and Ben

Jonson were discovering and revealing the magic possible in English phrasing; just at the time when the English language as we know it was taking its essential form; just when thought in England was incandescent and literary art aflame. Two or three generations later the 'King James' version of the Bible grew out of the same national-literary movement. Tyndale had led the way toward it almost a century before. Between Tyndale and the translation of 1611 came the Prayer Book, making the ancient forms of devotion live anew in noble English sentences, expressing no less nobly the ideals and the hopes that had come to birth in these more recent days. Not only the Episcopal Church, but the whole English-speaking world, remains 'bound together by the Prayer Book'; for without the *Book of Common Prayer* the English language would by no means have become what it is.

With the language goes the sense of nationality, of fellow-membership in an integrated community, which the sixteenth century brought to realization and which the succeeding years have confirmed. Go where one will throughout the world, the English Church is the rallying point for British people. The writer's parents were married in the Anglican Cathedral at Shanghai; and the vows they took were just those that two of his young friends repeated a few months ago at St. Clement's Church in Berkeley, California.

The Holy Communion is administered at Ram Allah in Palestine with the same words of administration as are used regularly in the Chapel of Mills College. Easter services in the Cathedral of St. George in Jerusalem, and those in the Cathedral of St. John the Divine in New York, are essentially the same. Morning Prayer in mid-Pacific and mid-Atlantic, in the Bay of Bengal and in the Mediter-ranean, is the same form of prayer as is used by the folk at home in every local parish Church, and provides the same feeling of being at home wherever one may be. Captain Scott read from the Prayer Book on the Antarctic plateau, and Sir John Franklin far in the Arctic Ocean, and so have hundreds of unknown Britons in Central Africa and on the Canadian prairie. Do things of this sort matter? They do matter, to countless thousands who need to feel at home, who need to know that they belong.

The Englishness of the Church is responsible for yet an-other of its normative qualities: that is, its lack of primary interest in theological dispute. It broke from Rome on the incident of Henry's marital affairs, but by the essence of the growing spirit of English independence that was not to be denied. There was therefore no theological quarrel basically involved. The quarrel at the outset was adminis-trative only, and the separation from Rome has remained an administrative one. As a result there has been little in-clination to stress theological conformity as a condition of membership or of association. As England developed personal political freedom within the framework of her monarchical state, so she achieved personal religious free-dom within the fellowship of her monarchically-centered Church.

But this brings us directly to the other side of the Church of England's shield: a side which might be considered op-posite, yet which is necessary to complete the whole. The Church of England is authentically English. It is no less truly Catholic. That is, it is both a national Church and a universal Church: a Church that is universal in its ancient origins, that is universal too in its present inclusiveness.

The catholicity of the Anglican temper is abundantly illustrated in the regular forms of service. The customary, every-Sunday usage of the Anglican Churches in Morning Prayer draws upon the pre-Christian Book of the Jewish Psalms; the Jewish, Judaeo-Christian and Greek Christian Scriptures; the Eastern Orthodox Churches of the second and fourth centuries A.D.; the Gallican Church of the fifth century, and the Roman in the sixth; and the reformers of the sixteenth and seventeenth centuries. The American Prayer Book of 1929 adds new prayers expressive of twentieth-century needs and aspirations, and phrased in terms of twentieth-century concepts.

It is the special genius of Anglicanism to draw into itself whatever it has found to be true and honorable, lovely and of good report: whatever it has found, and wherever it may have found it. In the same spirit of catholicity, in the same feeling of unity with the continuing and universal Church of the ages, both the British and the American Churches have entered into active fellowship with the Orthodox Churches of Eastern Europe and Western Asia. Roman Catholicism, by being specifically Roman, has denied its universality to some. English Catholicism, while remaining English, has opened its doors to all who will enter.

Here is the meaning, and herein is the positive value, of the quip about 'agreement to disagree.' It took more than a century, indeed, for England to arrive at this position. Under Edward VI the new national Church caused the execution of Roman Catholics; and so it was not surprising

that in the Catholic reaction under Queen Mary there occurred the martyrdom of Protestants. The Puritans, rising
to power in the 1640s, dipped their hands in the blood not
only of King Charles I but also of his Archbishop Laud of
Canterbury. It was perhaps a lucky accident, religiously as
well as politically, that forty years later James II made
himself so hated by almost everyone in England that he was
dethroned by a revolutionary movement whose members
represented every shade of political and theological opinion. The new order these revolutionists established in 1689
was driven to tolerance by its own inner variousness; and
from that year on tolerance has held the field.

Thus the state Church of England has had to house ritu-
alists and anti-ritualists, sacramentarians and anti-sacramen-
tarians, mystics and men of action, literalists and symbol-
ists, pronounced Socialists such as the late and lamented
Archbishop Temple and economic conservatives of equal
eminence and equal enthusiasm. That the Church has
housed all these varieties adequately, and on the whole happily, more than two centuries and a half bear witness. Both
Labourites and Tories sit as Bishops in the House of Lords.
High Churchmen and Low Churchmen argue about the
place of the altar and the character of its ornaments, but
neither thinks to deny the other access to that altar. Modernism holds the field in the English Universities, a kind
of fundamentalism in some of the missionary enterprises.
The writer has been scolded by Anglicans both for turning eastward to say the Creed, and for not genuflecting
when he said it; yet both these Anglicans regard the Creed
as important. They, and all the millions of people taking
positions in between them, remain members not only of

the Church as institution, but also of the Church as fellow-ship.

Here the ancient ritual plays its major part as agent of spiritual oneness. Its practice varies from the casual and almost stark to the elaborate and lavishly colorful. Its words convey many varying things to those who say them. Its antiquity and its mood mean more than do its words and its gestures. They mean historic continuity. They mean long experience and eager thinking and profound feeling. They mean belonging, and belonging together. They mean, that is to say, the keeping of the unity of the spirit in the bond of peace.

It may be that the alleged lukewarmness of the Episcopal mood is an expression of this tolerance in fellowship, which time and necessity forced upon the Episcopal institution. Someone remarked recently that 'Nothing in England is adequately heated: not even an argument.' There is some truth in that; and if it means that arguments within Anglicanism, by sacrificing heat, generate some measure of light, then the coolness is not wholly to be scorned. Where we disagree, we may agree to differ; and thereby we are set free to live together and to work together on what remains to us as common ground.

The whole state of Christ's Church can be served no other wise. Did we divide on details of ritual usage, we would have at least as many denominations as we have local Churches. Did we excommunicate on shades of theological judgment, we would have as many communions as we have persons. England has shown that a national state can endure, and can be an effective unity, while it debates and votes and changes its procedures with the times. The Church of England has shown that a Church can endure, can be a truly Catholic fellowship, can serve man in its united worshipping of God, while demanding that the individual shall think for himself and be himself within it. Fearing God and honoring the King, the Church honors also all men, and loves the brotherhood.

More truly than they knew, Cranmer and Latimer and Ridley lighted a candle in England that shall not be put out. That candle has flickered often, and it never has turned into a bonfire. But it shines into many a dark place, and it has given light to uncounted millions of men and women. We may believe that its light will brighten earth's darkness for long years to come, and for many millions of people more. 'Let us pray for the whole state of Christ's Church.'

VII

'SO TRUTH BE IN THE FIELD'

(The Congregationalists)

'Ye know that the princes of the Gentiles exercise domin-
ion over them, and they that are great exercise authority
upon them. But it shall not be so among you.'
—St. Matthew 20:25f (AV).

'Let the Church rule in spirituall wise, and not in worldlie
maner; by a liuelie lawe preached, and not by a ciuill lawe
written.'—Robert Browne, *A Treatise of Reformation*
without Tarrying for Anie, A.D. 1582.

'The magistrate, by virtue of his office, is not to meddle
with religion, or matters of conscience, nor to compel
men to this or that form of religion or doctrine, but to
leave the Christian religion to the free conscience of
every one.'—John Smythe, *Confession*, A.D. 1612.

'Who ever knew Truth put to the wors, in a free and open
encounter?'—John Milton, *Areopagitica: A Speech for*
the Liberty of Unlicenc'd Printing, A.D. 1644.

'The first human subject and original of civil power is the
people. . . . When they are free, they may set up what
species of government they please.'—John Wise, *A Vin-*
dication of the Government of New England Churches,
A.D. 1717.

Two quite external facts illustrate the nature of the religious grouping that forms the subject of this chapter.

The first is the matter of official names. We have had occasion hitherto to notice the Roman Catholic *Church*, the *Church* of England, the Protestant Episcopal *Church*, the Presbyterian *Church*. We shall turn soon to the *Society* of Friends, and thence to the Methodist *Church*. Those all are the legal names of the bodies concerned. Each great Church just mentioned thinks of itself in the singular; and so also does the Quaker organization, though it prefers to call itself a 'Society.' But there is no such thing as 'the Congregational *Church*' as a national institution. The fellowship to which American Congregationalists belong is quite deliberately named 'The National Council of Congregational and Christian Church*es*.' Congregationalism is a plural matter: and that is just what makes it 'Congregational.'

The second typical datum is that there is no single word, spelled with a capital letter, which precisely identifies all the members of the religious communities now to be considered. Their records and statistics have to be looked up under five different headings at least: those of Baptists, Congregationalists, Disciples, Unitarians, and Universalists. This is another symptom of plurality. Even the word 'Congregational,' indicating separation as it does, is not enough to include all the separate forms that have developed within the general Congregational tradition. Two others of these groups, the Baptists and the Disciples of Christ, have played so large and honored a part in American religious history, and count so many adherents today, that in the present study they rightly claim separate chapters for themselves.

There are indeed two historic words which are inclusive enough to cover all five of the denominations in the 'Congregational' category. But they are words which have been little used in the past century, except by Church historians; and many who belong to the groups in question would not at all recognize themselves as 'Independents' or 'Separatists' (at least not with a capital 'I' or a capital 'S').

'Separatism' and 'Independency' none the less were familiar terms in the religious discussions and realignments of the sixteenth and seventeenth centuries. It will be remembered that after the Church of England separated itself from Rome, there arose a very strong Calvinist (Presbyterian) movement within the national Church: a movement which became dominant in Oliver Cromwell's Commonwealth, and whose influence never quite has disappeared. The Calvinists wanted to reform the whole Church according to their own ideas, and for a time they succeeded in doing so.

There were in England other Protestants who were not content with attempting reformation inside the existing Church. They were not reformers, but strictly revolutionists. They wanted not to improve the Church of England, which they considered hopeless, but rather to do away with it. Their first leader and spokesman was one Robert Browne, a clergyman of the established Church who rejected the authority of the Bishops, and who in 1582 published what he called *A Treatise of Reformation without Tarrying for Anie*. Browne and his congregation were hounded by the officials of Elizabeth's regime, and for some time sought safety by meeting each week in a different place. After fifty-six of them had been imprisoned and three executed, the remnant took refuge in Holland.

Other English congregations followed their example. One such, from the town of Gainsborough in Lincolnshire, was led by a minister named John Smythe. Reaching Holland in 1606, Smythe met there a number of Mennonites, whose pacifist and pietist group had originated in Germany in the sixteenth century. By 1609 Smythe had been persuaded by their arguments against the baptizing of babies. (The point of course was that being a Christian was a matter of voluntary, individual choice, and so could not be determined for anyone by anyone else. It followed that baptism, as the symbol of personal acceptance of the Christian faith, should be postponed until the individual was old enough to decide for himself.)

Smythe and his associates formed in Holland the first English Baptist Church. Later Smythe took the further step of actually joining the Mennonites, but at this point most of his followers repudiated him. In 1612 the Gainsborough Church returned to England, still Baptist in opinion and usage and name, and Baptist Churches have been active and successful there ever since. Fifty years later they gave to the nation and the world John Bunyan, author of *The Pilgrim's Progress*. The history of the Baptists in America, and the place they have made for themselves here, will concern us in the chapter which follows this one.

Another Separatist congregation, whose minister was John Robinson, fled from Scrooby in Nottinghamshire to Amsterdam, and thence moved to Leyden. Robinson laid special stress on the congregation's right to choose its own minister from within its own ranks, or from elsewhere if it wished, without appointment by any outside authority and without need of prior ordination. After twelve years this Scrooby congregation, seeking a new economic chance and a personal freedom for which there was no room in crowded Holland, arranged to settle in the New World within the area chartered to the Virginia Company. These were the Mayflower Pilgrims, whose landing on Cape Cod in 1620 marked the beginning of Congregationalism in America.

The Separatists had been assailed and persecuted both by the Episcopal and by the Presbyterian parties within the Church of England from the time of Elizabeth. As the Stuart Kings James I and Charles I swung definitely away from Presbyterianism, the Presbyterians began to find themselves persecuted too. Charles' Archbishop of Canterbury, William Laud, exerted heavy pressure on these reformers, now commonly called 'Puritans.' While in England the conflict took its course toward open civil war, many of the Puritans decided to imitate the Separatists and migrate to America. Between 1628 and 1640 not less than 20,000 of these people crossed the Atlantic and settled in what became the Massachusetts Bay Colony, immediately to the north of the Plymouth Colony of Separatists.

The Puritans kept their Calvinist, determinist theology, but in their new setting they had neither opportunity nor motive to maintain the structure of the Church of England. Following the Separatist example of their Pilgrim neighbors at Plymouth, they set up their Churches on a Congregational scheme of government. When later the two colonies were united, the Calvinist majority determined the dominant theological attitudes of the people of Massachusetts. Thus the Churches of New England became characteristically Congregational in structure but Calvinist in teaching, and remained so through the eighteenth century.

Congregational rule meant absolute freedom for the

local Church to do as it wished; but it by no means accorded equal liberty to the individual member of the congregation. In effect and in law the local New England Churches were the state Churches of their respective townships, setting up in each of them a religious rule as rigid as that of Calvin in Geneva. Those who carried rebellion on into personal attitudes were forced out. Thus the enquiring Roger Williams was driven from Salem, Massachusetts, and founded the new and genuinely free settlement of 'Rhode Island and Providence Plantations.' Thus also the liberal Thomas Hooker moved to the valley of the Connecticut, and at Hartford began the life of yet another American commonwealth.

Meanwhile in England the war between Parliament and King, which had begun as a war between Puritans and Episcopalians, became confused by conflict between Presbyterians and Separatists within the Parliamentary forces. In Cromwell's army Separatism was largely associated with social radicalism, represented in the so-called 'Levellers' and 'Diggers.' The active mind of John Milton, starting from a base of Episcopalian training at Cambridge, moved on through Presbyterianism to Independency; and as now we know, through the discovery of his unpublished treatise *On Christian Doctrine*, finally into something very like later Unitarianism.

The Presbyterians, victorious at the time over their Episcopal rivals, sought to guarantee their position by strict control including a stringent censorship of publications. Milton, whose unhappy personal life had made him acutely radical on the subject of divorce, resisted the dictation of the new majority just as with its members formerly he had defied the Bishops. Rising far above his immediate and personal reason for writing, he published in 1644 his *Areopagitica: A Speech for the Liberty of Unlicenc'd Printing*. (True to the principle for which he argued, he issued it without having submitted it to the censors for scrutiny and licence.)

The *Areopagitica* moves beyond the religious disputes of the day, and beyond the quarrels of contending sects, to declare the virtue and need of absolute freedom of personal expression in all realms.

Though all the windes of doctrin (it urges) were let loose to play upon the earth, so Truth be in the field, we do injuriously by licencing and prohibiting to misdoubt her strength. Let her and Falshood grapple; who ever knew Truth put to the wors, in a free and open encounter?

Two years after the *Areopagitica* came the extended sonnet, 'On the new Forcers of Conscience under the Long Parliament,' with its biting last line, '*New Presbyter* is but *Old Priest* writ Large.' Six years later still, hoping that Cromwell would go yet further than he had in supporting the Separatists and suppressing the Presbyterians, Milton addressed to the Protector a sonnet which moves from praise of former military success to a plea for present action:

Cromwell our Chief of men, that through a Croud,
Not of War only, but distractions rude;
Guided by Faith, and Matchless Fortitude:
To Peace and Truth, thy Glorious way hast Plough'd . . .
         . . . yet much remains
To Conquer still; Peace hath her Victories
No less than those of War; new Foes arise
Threatning to bind our Souls in Secular Chains,

Help us to save Free Conscience from the paw
Of Hireling Wolves, whose Gospel is their Maw.

The freedom thus sought by the now Independent Milton was continued in the practice of the Independent Churches: and so was the quarreling that went with it. To the existing Congregational and Baptist fellowships there was added late in the eighteenth century the Unitarian, separating from the others in insisting on the absolute unity of God and therefore in denying the special divinity of Jesus. At about the same time there came into being yet another movement, which was called 'Universalist' because it held that all men and women ultimately would be reconciled to God, and so that there could be no eternal punishment.

The latest major offshoot of Independency, the Disciples of Christ or 'the Christian Church,' appeared in the early nineteenth century under the leadership of the naturalized American Alexander Campbell. Its history and special character will be noted in a subsequent chapter. One branch of this 'Christian' fellowship recently joined the National Council of Congregational Churches, but the larger number of Disciples have remained apart, and constitute two separate national organizations.

There are in the world today some twelve million members in all the Independent Churches, of whom about ten million are in the United States and most of the others in England. The Baptists are much the most numerous single group, with over seven and a half million members in this country, but they are divided into several separate denominational units. The Disciples number just over a million, the Congregationalists almost as many. The 'Churches of Christ,' now distinct from the Disciples, have about three hundred thousand members. There are some sixty thousand Unitarians, and about forty-six thousand Universalists.

What are the twelve million Independents like? What have they contributed to our religious life and to our cultural pattern? Their great gift obviously is that reflected in their name: their devotion to independence of thought and action, their stress upon 'the free conscience of every one,' upon the right of 'free people' to 'set up what species of government they please.'

Religious liberty among the Independents pointed the way toward liberty in all of life. Just as John Milton, in defying Presbyterian censorship, was led to make the classic plea for absolute freedom of speech, so in the next century John Wise's *Vindication of the Government of New England Churches* became one of the historic defences of the democratic process in all fields, secular as well as religious. The New England town meeting, commonly recognized as the fountainhead of American democratic practice, is directly related to and largely dependent on the congregational meeting in which the Separatists determined their religious procedures by majority vote. In early New England, indeed, town and congregation were identical in their memberships; and so inevitably town and congregation, as organizations, ran their affairs in the same way.

It would not be accurate to say that every Congregational group has been really hospitable to new ideas, or willing to grant full liberty of expression to dissenters. A local Church as well as a national one can crystallize theologically and institutionally; and even a loose fellowship can be hard on those who depart far from its accepted ways. That is why we have in this country, operating under the Congregational form, not one historic major denomination, but five.

Yet the habit of freedom often does carry over, as it did with Milton and with Roger Williams, from congregational into individual choice of values. On the whole there has been less heresy-hunting within the congregational Churches than in those more closely organized. (Thus, for example, Harry Emerson Fosdick could not satisfy the Presbytery of New York as to his orthodoxy, but gets along in full comfort as minister of the self-governing Riverside Baptist Church.) And the fact that each local Church is a law unto itself makes it fairly easy for anyone, dissatisfied with the creed or the customs of one congregation, to find another whose views he shares enough to be a cordial, participating member of it.

Local autonomy has made also for amazing diversity even within what we call a single 'denomination.' In the writer's student days there were in Boston (as of course there still are) two big downtown Congregational Churches. At Park Street Church, called 'Brimstone Corner' because of the burning antislavery sermons delivered there in the nineteenth century, Dr. A. Z. Conrad kept the name appropriate by his preaching of a fiery fundamentalism. Old South Church, however, under the ministry of Dr. George A. Gordon, was liberal to the point of what then was called 'modernism.' The two congregations were satisfied, each with its own minister and each with its own interpretation of Christianity; and that was all that Congregationalism asked.

The same degree of variety exists as to customs in worship. Usually the Sunday services are dignified, but scarcely ornate. The average usage of the larger Unitarian and Congregational Churches on the two coasts tends toward an increasing emphasis on ritual. The Midwest is in general much more informal, much nearer to the sharp anti-ceremonialism of the early Puritans and Separatists. At the other extreme is King's Chapel in Boston, an Episcopal Church which by vote of its members became Unitarian in 1782. It has kept the entire ancient ritual, except that it avoids any open reference to the Holy Trinity; and its service as a result is almost as elaborate as that in any Anglican or Roman Catholic Church.

Two trends are apparent in the life of Congregationalism today. One is toward unity among the several fellowships, the other toward closer organization and more decisive leadership within each Congregational denomination. Each of these reflects a swing away from the extremes of Independent emphasis as they worked in the past. The Unitarians and Universalists some time ago effected a considerable unity of interests and activities; though recently, it is reported, the Universalists have turned rather toward union with the larger and more traditional Protestant bodies. In New England one often hears the phrase, 'the two branches of Congregationalism,' meaning the Congregationalists and the Unitarians; and it is clear that the theological dispute on which those Churches parted would divide few of them now. Part of the 'Christian' fellowship, as was pointed out above, now has joined forces with the Congregational, though most of it has remained apart.

Within the denominations, despite their theory of separation and local autonomy, common interests have forced united action and so the development of overhead organization. Each of them has its own publishing house, each its own colleges and theological schools, each its own type of missionary enterprise: and so each has had to raise its central funds and to maintain its fund-raising agencies. Alexander Campbell himself, who as leader of the Disciples had begun by decrying all organization on any scale larger than that of the local Church, finished by creating the American Christian Missionary Society and himself serving as its President for fourteen years. Regional leadership is exercised by general officers variously titled, but apparently becoming all of them more positive in their influence on local activities.

The reason for these trends toward unity and closer organization is easy to see. Left to itself and in its unmixed form, Independency very easily turns into anarchy. That is obvious as to persons: as witness Milton's swing across the arc of religious radicalism, and Roger Williams' self-separation from the Separatists of Massachusetts (and later from the Baptists of Providence as well), and the number of Unitarians who recently have gone on from believing in a single God to believing in no God at all. It is also clear that a local congregation needs, and ultimately comes to want, a wider fellowship than its own neighborhood can provide. Just as the Churches with episcopal and presbyterian forms of government have become more democratic with the passing of time, so the congregationally-organized Churches have moved toward a more definite and a more general discipline.

The balancing of these factors of order and freedom is a crucial problem not only for Church government and teaching, but also for all our life together. The groups studied before these laid the larger emphasis on tradition and authority; and it was natural that some people would react from their attitude as the Separatists did. The next chapters will examine two other and somewhat different protests against overhead control, as they developed among the Baptists and the Quakers; and then we shall consider the Methodists, who represent a return to authority and toward universality.

From where we stand, it is easy for us to see the divisiveness and weakness that marked Independency in its early days. The present Independents have seen these difficulties too, and are moving to correct the extreme consequences of their principles of freedom. There remain very great and positive contributions from early Separatism, and from modern Congregationalism, in the total stream of the Christian tradition.

The Separatists have challenged us to enquire freely and to speak bravely. All of them in their beginnings dared public misunderstanding and hatred, in their devotion to truth as they saw it. Each group of them has given us its own glimpses of truth that had not yet come in at our own casements: the New Englanders in their self-validating governments; the Baptists in their demand for personal activity rather than passive acceptance; the Unitarians in a theological impact that has changed the thinking of us all; the Universalists in a love for all men which they could not but assign to God; the Disciples in direct Christian simplicity; recent Congregationalists in their pioneering of

Christian action in economics and in social relations. Ever we see, in the history of the Independents and in their life, their compelling faith that Truth is mighty and will prevail; that when Truth and Falsehood grapple in free and open encounter, Truth is not put to the worse.

'So Truth be in the field,' the Independent yet insists, Truth ultimately must win. Discussion and controversy and even dissension may be necessary means to our discovering of Truth. If we do believe in Truth's power, we shall not fear the challenge of the Independent mind. If we seek Truth as the goal, we shall claim and use our own freedom of enquiry too.

VIII

'BELIEVERS ARE THE SUBJECTS'
(The Baptists)

'*John did baptize in the wilderness, and preach the baptism of repentance for the remission of sins.*'
—St. Mark 1:4 (AV).

'*He that believeth and is baptized shall be saved; but he that believeth not shall be damned.*'—St. Mark 16:16 (AV).

'*Whatever worship, ministry, ministration, the best and purest are practiced without faith and true persuasion that they are the true institutions of God, they are sin, sinful worships, ministries, etc.*'—Roger Williams, *The Bloody Tenent of Persecution for Cause of Conscience*, A.D. 1644.

'*All the Members hereof shall for ever enjoy full free Absolute and uninterrupted Liberty of Conscience.*'—Charter of Rhode Island College (now Brown University), 1764.

'*We believe Baptism and the Lord's Supper are ordinances of Jesus Christ and that Believers are the Subjects of these Ordinances and the true mode of Baptism is by Immersion.*'—Records of the Forks of Elkhorn Baptist Church, Kentucky, 2nd Saturday in December 1803.

IT IS an old joke that the Bible reports the work of 'John the Baptist' but knows nothing of any 'John the Methodist.' There is an important historical point implied here:

namely, that the Baptists have unquestionable foundation in the New Testament for the two special emphases that have marked them as distinct from most other denominations, and that have fixed their name. It is evident that John baptized only adults, men (and perhaps women) who themselves repented of their sins and on their own behalf pledged themselves to the Kingdom of God as John preached it. It is also most probable that John's mode of baptism was that of immersion: 'in the river of Jordan' scarcely can mean anything else, and the Gospel references to Jesus' 'coming up out of the water' are decisive as to the way in which the early Church pictured the event.

The rite as administered by John roots in the ceremonial washings prescribed by Jewish law. It is possible, though not at all certain, that John himself was influenced by the Jewish monastic sect of the Essenes, which flourished on the desert fringe of Palestine in the first centuries B.C. and A.D. Christian usage took up John's symbol, again necessarily first for those who themselves believed, and again at the outset using the mode of immersion. The tale of St. Philip and the Ethiopian eunuch, recorded in the eighth chapter of the Book of Acts, is as clear about their going 'down both into the water' as it is about the eunuch's own change of mind and heart.

Questions arise, however, as early as St. Paul's visit to Philippi on his second missionary journey. In the story of the jailer's baptism there is no reference to leaving the house to find sufficient water, and the baptizing not only of the jailer but also of 'all his' raises not only the question as to whether any young children were involved, but also the more serious one as to the extent to which other members of the family exercised their own personal choice.

Later in St. Paul's career baptism seems already to have moved into an external and magical as distinct from an inward and personal realm, in that practice of 'baptism for the dead' which St. Paul mentions as prevailing in Corinth and which he makes no attempt to oppose. In the second century St. Irenaeus argued for infant baptism, as necessary to ensure salvation in case of early death, and soon afterward Origen contended that the apostles had practised it.

Along with the magical virtue assigned to the rite, there arose the belief that sin committed after baptism could not be forgiven. On this ground many careful souls chose to postpone their baptism as long as possible. Among these was Constantine, the first 'Christian Emperor.' He was baptized on his deathbed; and it seems that he had taken full advantage of the liberty previously available.

Infant baptism, and the use of small amounts of water in pouring or sprinkling, became standard in the Western Church. Early in Reformation days there began to appear groups whom their opponents called 'Anabaptists,' or re-baptizers. Rejecting infant baptism as improper and therefore invalid, these sects demanded the baptism of all who chose to join them, including those who already had been christened in the traditional way. Enthusiasts and extremists on this point, the Anabaptists tended to extremes in other matters as well. Many of them rejected all authority, religious or civil, and some of these went beyond independence of mind into irresponsibility and even licentiousness of conduct.

Not only orthodox Catholics, but also the more cautious reformers, were greatly shocked by these phenomena. The Anabaptists were involved in that Peasants' Revolt which

Martin Luther so vigorously condemned, and their vaga-
ries served as an excuse for the cruellest Spanish repression
of all Protestants in the Netherlands. A moderating influence appeared with Menno Simon, father of the 'Mennonites,' who shared the Anabaptist conviction against
infant baptism, but who insisted upon the most rigid discipline in personal behavior.

With John Smythe's adoption in 1609 of Mennonite
views, noted in the preceding chapter, there begins the
history of the Baptist denomination properly so called.
The first Baptists were 'Arminian' in theology, stressing
free will and believing that salvation was available to all
men; they therefore called themselves 'General Baptists.'
In the 1630s several groups of English Presbyterians, concluding that infant baptism was unscriptural, broke from
their fellows and organized Baptist Churches which maintained the Calvinistic doctrine of the special 'election' of
the saved. These became known as 'Particular Baptists,'
and continue in the Primitive ('hardshell') Baptists of today. It was not until the 1640s that the Baptists came generally to insist upon immersion as the only proper mode
of administering the rite.

It is a curious fact, but a significant one, that the greatest
hero of the Baptist movement in America, and the founder
of the first Baptist Church in this country, was himself officially a Baptist for not more than four months of his life.
Roger Williams, a Cambridge man who in 1630 left England seeking liberty of conscience, failed to find it in the
Massachusetts Bay Colony. Settled as minister in Salem,
Williams was charged with 'Separatist' heresy because he
opposed a compulsory oath of allegiance to the colonial

government. In 1635 he was sentenced to exile, and early in 1636 was scheduled for deportation to England.

Three days before the arrival of the necessary warrant, he disappeared. During an earlier sojourn in the Plymouth Colony, which was somewhat less insistent on conformity than was its neighbor to the north, Williams had made friends with some of the Narragansett Indians. They now gave him shelter through the rest of the winter. In the spring four friends joined him, and soon came other sympathizers from Salem. A settlement at Sekonk, within the bounds of the Plymouth Colony, had to be abandoned because of Massachusetts Bay pressure on Governor Winslow. West of the Sekonk River Williams tried again, buying land from the Indians and establishing the 'plantations of Providence.'

The settlement received increasing numbers of Williams' followers from Salem, and soon began to attract others who wanted total freedom of conscience. The Pequot Indians were fought off, with the Narragansetts lending covert aid to the settlers, and with Williams displaying some ability as a military strategist. Providence began to govern itself through a 'covenant' agreed to by about twenty persons. A new compact in 1640 provided for details of administration on a broadly democratic base. In order to safeguard the Providence holdings from English and other adventurers Williams at last, in 1644, yielded to authority enough to seek and to secure a Parliamentary charter.

A neighboring community took root on Aquidneck Island, under the leadership of John Clarke and other friends of Williams. In 1654, after numerous disputes and adjustments, the two settlements were united and Williams was elected President of the Colony. Reëlected in 1655 and 1656, he found himself driven toward a centralizing of authority which ran counter to his own principles of absolute freedom. A final charter, granted by Charles II in 1663 to 'Rhode Island and Providence Plantations,' and appointing Benedict Arnold as the first Governor, with the provision that his successors should be chosen by free election, served as the colonial and state constitution until 1842. (There was no Rhode in 'Rhode Island.' The name is a corruption of 'Roode Eylandt,' as the Dutch fishermen called the 'red island' of Aquidneck.)

Meanwhile Williams turned, after one brief experiment in religious organization, to total freedom and independence in his own religious life. Already in Salem he had been accused of 'Anabaptistry,' a condemnatory label about as vague and as fear-provoking to the average Puritan then as is that of 'Communism' to some minds today. Early in 1639 Williams was indeed persuaded to the Baptist view, possibly by Catherine Hutchinson, sister of the more famous Anne. He was baptized ('rebaptized') in March of that year by one Ezekiel Holliman, or Holyman, and in turn himself baptized Holliman and ten others. Thus was established the First Baptist Church of Providence, the earliest in the United States, with Williams as its minister.

The restless mind of Roger Williams, however, could not tarry there. He began to doubt the validity of all the Christian ordinances, on the ground that manifest corruption in the mediaeval Church had broken the true apostolic succession. (It is interesting to find a Baptist thus concerned with the apostolic succession; but it is in character that his conclusion was negative.) In June or July of 1639

Roger Williams laid down his pastorate and withdrew from membership in the Church.

Nevertheless he maintained cordial relationship with it, and with his successors who did not share his scruples. Becoming in name what always he had been in fact, a 'Seeker,' Williams continued to doubt and to enquire for the rest of his life. Thirty-seven years after this episode of temporary Baptist membership, and eight years before he died, Williams wrote in his reply to George Fox (*George Fox Digged Out of His Burrowes*),

I profess that if my soul could find rest in joining unto any of the churches professing Christ Jesus now extant, I would readily and gladly do it, yea, unto themselves whom I now opposed.

Providence and Rhode Island continued to be dominantly and characteristically Baptist in leadership and tradition. The Church at Newport, founded by John Clarke in 1641, was explicitly Baptist at least as early as 1648. Rhode Island College, established in the town of Warren principally through the energies of the Philadelphia Association (of Baptist Churches), had a majority of Baptist trustees, but from the outset included on its board also Congregationalists, Quakers, and even Anglicans, in harmony with its charter's promise of 'full free Absolute and uninterrupted Liberty of Conscience.' (The College was moved to Providence in 1770, and in 1804 was renamed 'Brown University' in honor of Nicholas Brown, an alumnus of 1786 and a most generous benefactor.) To this day the Baptist Churches are in Providence what the Congregational are in Boston, the normative Christian bodies and the carriers of local religious tradition; and to this day the Commencement exercises of Brown University are conducted in the First Baptist Meeting House of Providence.

Baptist believers went to the other colonies too. In Pennsylvania, New Jersey, and Delaware, they found a ready welcome from the tolerant Quakers, even though Williams had written at his bitterest in the controversy with George Fox; and it was in Philadelphia that the first Association of Baptist Churches was organized in 1707. The earliest Baptist Church in Maine was founded in 1682 under the leadership of one William Screven, son of a signer of the English Baptist Confession of 1656. Official pressure forced Screven's departure, and a year or so later we find him organizing the first of the Baptist Churches in the South, that at Somerton, South Carolina. In Massachusetts opposition continued furiously for a time, but faded away by the end of the seventeenth century. The 'Great Awakening' of the early eighteenth century was chiefly Congregational (Jonathan Edwards) and Methodist (George Whitefield), but the Baptists profited greatly by the general quickening of religious interest, and carried on the revivalist tradition after some of their precursors had moved far away from it.

An attempt in the Virginia legislature to make infant baptism legally compulsory drew attention to the Baptist point of view, and soon created sympathy for Baptist defenders of the minority conscience. Patrick Henry's opposition to the Anglican clergy became involved with the Baptist issue, as it was with the developing political revolutionism of the colonies. When in 1779 the Church of England was disestablished in Virginia, the Baptist Churches added to their membership many former Anglicans, and thus gained their first firm foothold in the American South.

Independency persisted as a habit of mind. Rhode Island, ever suspicious of strong central power, sent no delegates to the Constitutional Convention of 1787, and ratified the new Federal Constitution reluctantly and under economic pressure only in 1790, a year after it had gone into effect. At the beginning of the nineteenth century, with a hundred thousand members all told, the Baptists were divided into six independent denominations. Thirteen decades later, with almost eight million members in the United States, they counted twenty-one separate organizational bodies. To the winning of the West they brought personal conviction, tremendous enthusiasm, and an evident passion for argument; but no less they contributed a moral passion and a stern group discipline which did much to set the cultural tone of the whole area from the Alleghenies to the foothills of the Rockies, and so to establish that authentic American pattern which belongs to the Midwest.

On the spreading frontier Baptist unconventionality and individualism found a congenial soil. Scriptural arguments for believer's baptism and for immersion were highly effective in a culture which took for granted both the Bible's literal accuracy and its absolute authority. The records of the Forks of Elkhorn Baptist Church in Kentucky, made available in our time by the appreciative and scholarly work of William Warren Sweet, and the source of this chapter's title, provide abundant illustration of early western Baptist attitudes and activities.

Literal Biblicism had led this Church, along with a number of other frontier groups, to observe the Sabbath on the seventh day of the week. (There are still some seven thousand Seventh Day Baptists, not to be confused with the

Seventh Day Adventists, in the United States.) After each Saturday's service the Forks of Elkhorn Church held a business meeting. Members were admitted 'by Experience and Baptism,' and others were granted 'letters of Dismission.' 'Mr. Garnets Sue,' presumably a slave, was 'excluded for lying Tattling and unguarded conversation,' Theodore Bowler for 'immoral conduct and not hearing the Church,' a startling number of brothers, and a few sisters, for 'Drinking to an excess.'

The frontier Churches included both slaves and slaveholders within their fellowship. As the slavery issue became acute, however, sides were taken and the lines were sharply drawn. On the second Saturday in September 1807, at the Forks of Elkhorn Church,

Bro. William Hickman came forward and informed the Church that he was distressed on account of the practice of Slavery as being tolerated by the members of the Baptist Society, therefore declared himself no more in Union with us, or the Elkhorn Association— Therefore the Church considers him no more a member in fellowship.

Bro. Plewright Sisk withdrew for the same reason on the same day. A fortnight earlier there had been formed the first 'Friends of Humanity Association,' composed of churches and ministers refusing fellowship with slaveholders. The movement continued small in Kentucky, but grew to large proportions in Illinois. The First African Baptist Church in Savannah, Georgia, had been established in 1787, and in 1830 the first Negro Baptist Association, bearing the name of 'Providence,' was organized in Ohio. Northern and Southern Baptists split decisively on the slavery question in 1845, and the two Conventions still remain apart. The Negro Baptist Churches, organized in two national bodies, today have more than three and a half million members, almost equalling the total of the two great 'white' organizations.

Protestant foreign missionary work from English-speaking lands had been pioneered by the English Baptist William Carey in India, where he labored from 1793 to 1834. The American Board of Commissioners for Foreign Missions, dominantly Congregational but at first including also Presbyterians and Friends, was organized in 1810. In 1812 the American Board sent to Burma two young volunteers of the 'haystack mission,' Adoniram Judson and Luther Rice. On the long voyage Judson and Rice read the Bible, and found themselves persuaded to Baptist views. While Judson remained in Burma, Rice returned to the United States to create a missionary society in support of a Baptist missionary already in the field. The fruit of this effort was not only the American Baptist Foreign Missionary Union, but also the first National Convention of Baptist Churches (1814).

A unique phenomenon in American Christian history was the rise of the 'Anti-Mission Baptists,' whose movement divided many of the Churches and Associations on the frontier from the third to the fifth decades of the century. The basic cause of opposition to missionary activity (both foreign and home) probably was the old Baptist suspicion of centralized authority. A secondary factor was distrust of a professional and educated ministry, which of necessity the missionaries represented. Theological support for the position was found in the prevailing Calvinism of Baptists in the West, by reference to the divine choice of the 'elect,' and to God's power to save whom he would, without need of impertinent human efforts.

It is easy to accuse and to convict the Baptists of inconsistency. Inconsistency of the individual grew almost inevitably from the mood of persistent enquiry represented in Roger Williams. Inconsistency within the fellowship is encouraged both by the theory of absolute freedom and by the practice of congregational organization. While the Baptists had a monopoly of explicit and articulate 'antimissionism,' they also have been eager proponents, supporters, and operators of missionary enterprise. While many of their people have feared and opposed formal education, and some still do, others have built and conducted some of the most notable Colleges and Universities in the land: Brown, Bucknell, Chicago, Colby, only to start the alphabet. While Biblical literalism and frontier revivalism persist in many Baptist Churches, the Newton Theological Institution and the University of Chicago Divinity School have been in the forefront of exact and critical Biblical and theological scholarship, and Harry Emerson Fosdick proclaims his own version of liberal Christianity in a Baptist Church whose building is imitated from the Cathedral at Chartres. (As a clue to the trend, it is to be noted that both Newton and Chicago now are united with Congregational schools of theology, the former with Andover and the latter with Chicago Theological Seminary.)

Some American pseudo-sophisticates use the words 'Baptist' and 'Methodist' as terms of contempt, inferring lower-class mentality, attitudes, and habits. Rightly many Baptists and Methodists choose to regard this attempted slur as a compliment. The Baptists justly may claim that the common people have heard them gladly: which is why there are so many Baptists in America today. The major strength remains in the South, with a membership of more than two and a half million in the Southern Convention, plus the three and a half million Negro Baptists, as compared with fewer than a million and a half members (including a number of northern Negroes) in the Northern Convention. Most of the smaller groups, survivals of the early divisions, also are to be found in the southern and south central regions. The frontier tradition prevails in informality, and in a degree of sensationalism in some (though by no means all) of the larger city Churches. Everywhere there is earnest conviction, everywhere warm-hearted faith, everywhere a passion for service; and most important of all, there is everywhere the continuing insistence that each individual bears the responsibility for arriving at his own religious experience and faith.

'Believers are the subjects of these ordinances.' Yet the forms in which this emphasis is expressed have been (in some places) greatly modified with the passing of the years. 'Closed communion' now is the practice only of a small minority. Many Baptist Churches admit non-immersed persons as 'associate members,' and some of these Churches have in their active fellowship more 'associates' than regulars. Some time ago there was developed a Baptist ritual for the 'dedication of infants,' to meet the psychological need satisfied in other Churches in infant baptism, and ultimately recognized by some of the Baptist leaders themselves. It will occur to the reader that the equation thus becomes exact. Morally speaking, Baptist 'dedication of infants' equals christening in other communions, while confirmation or admission to full membership in those Churches equals Baptist 'believer's baptism.'

'He that believeth and is baptized shall be saved; and he that believeth not shall be damned'—whether or not he has been baptized, and to whatever family, to whatever tradition, he may trace his inheritance. If there is a difference of approach among the Independent groups, it is that while the Congregationalists tend to emphasize the content of independent thinking, the Baptists stress the principle of the individual's independence as such. The Baptist point, and the great Baptist gift to Christian thinking, is that each of us fixes his destiny on his own behalf, and no one of us for any other. The physical symbol gained perhaps undue attention in the days of formulation and controversy. The meaning and the value survive; and for that survival we have the Baptists largely to thank.

IX

'THE INNER LIGHT'

(The Quakers)

'Be still, and know that I am God.'—Psalm 46:10 (AV).

'Let your yea be yea; and your nay, nay.'
— St. James 5:12 (AV).

'I saw . . . that there was an ocean of darkness and death, but an infinite ocean of light and love which flowed over the ocean of darkness.'—George Fox, *Journal*, A.D. 1646.

'It is a most dangerous error, for a man to think to excuse himself in the breach of a moral duty, by a formal performance of worship.'—William Penn, *Fruits of Solitude*, No. 179, edition of 1726.

'In this Silence we learn abiding in the Divine will.'—John Woolman, *An Epistle to the Quarterly and Monthly Meetings of Friends*, A.D. 1772.

In the year 1650 a wandering and unauthorized preacher stood before Justice Bennet of Derby. To the judge's half-humorous chiding the prisoner, George Fox, replied, 'The time has come for even judges to quake and tremble before the Lord.' 'Ah,' said Justice Bennet, 'so you are Quakers, are you?'

The term caught the popular fancy, ever ready to giggle at what was new and different. Fox and his followers never objected to it strongly, for they did believe that men should have a healthy fear in the divine presence. And so they and their inheritors have been known as 'Quakers' ever since.

Their own first name for themselves was 'Children of Light,' based on one of Fox's favorite texts, 'Believe in the light, that ye may be the children of the light.' Later, when their numbers grew and a definite organization seemed to have become necessary, they came to use the designation, 'Society of Friends.' This has remained their official title through the years, though often they have added the phrase, 'commonly called Quakers.'

Light was George Fox's obsession. He was a mystic of the most intense sort, and phrased his mystical experience in terms of visual imagery. Evil was darkness. God revealed himself in light: 'an infinite ocean of light and love which flowed over the ocean of darkness.' Individualist mysticism of necessity found that light shining within the individual spirit: and so 'the inner light' became the criterion of all religious experience. (The exact phrase 'the inner light' seems not to have been used by Fox nor by any other of the early Quakers; but it is so apt a summary of their emphasis that it has become the standard symbol for the basic teaching and attitude of the Society of Friends.)

Fox began to preach during the years of the English Commonwealth, and so belongs to the general upsurge of protest against formalism both Anglican and Presbyterian: that is, against authority both churchly and doctrinal. He and his followers were persecuted by Anglicans and Presbyterians in accordance with the pattern of the time, and like so many minority groups seemed to thrive on persecution. They refused to conform to current usage as to clothes or language, they broke from prevailing 'law and order' in their rejecting of courtroom oaths and military service, they poured scorn on the ceremonies of the Churches (which Fox called 'steeple-houses') and on the pretensions of the ordained clergy.

They couldn't be driven into line, and they couldn't be bribed. 'Now I see,' Oliver Cromwell is reported to have said, 'that there is a people risen and come up that I cannot win either with gifts, honours, offices, or places.' The Stuart Restoration with Charles II brought a new tide of persecution, and some thirteen thousand Quakers went to prison during the early years of the new reign. Practical tolerance came in the 1670s, and the formal Act of Toleration after the accession of William and Mary in 1689. By the year 1700 there were sixty-six thousand Quakers in England, and at least half as many more in the American colonies.

The first Friends to invade the North American mainland, two women named Mary Fisher and Anne Austin, came from the West Indies to Boston in 1656. Boston still was permitting religious freedom only to its own Congregational-Calvinist majority. The Quaker interlopers were promptly imprisoned and soon deported, as were eight more who arrived five weeks later. The Colony passed special laws against the Quakers in 1656, 1657 and 1658, and three men and one woman were hanged on Boston Common. In 1673 King Charles, who had had enough of the persecutions in England, intervened in the interests of tolerance and mercy in Massachusetts; and at last in 1682 the Colony's anti-Quaker laws were repealed.

In England, meanwhile, an Admiral's son had come into contact with the Friends and had accepted their way of life. The Crown owed the Admiral a considerable sum of money, and in 1681 settled the debt by chartering to his son, William, a large area to the west of the colony of New Jersey. William Penn already had bought the proprietary rights to western New Jersey, and other Quakers had secured title to the eastern part of that settlement. Penn thought of calling his new territory 'Sylvania,' 'Woodland.' At the King's suggestion the proprietor's name was prefixed, and so 'Pennsylvania' came into being.

This was a haven for the Quakers; and, true to Quaker principles, it became a region of genuine religious freedom for all. Penn himself was at once a sincere believer and an able administrator. He set up a 'Frame of Government' which provided for a large degree of local self-government, and also for amendment at the will of the colonists themselves. He made a treaty with the Indians which Voltaire later was to describe as 'the only treaty that never was sworn to and never has been broken.' In the Colony grew up the first metropolis of North America, called 'Philadelphia,' the city of 'brotherly love'; and Philadelphia and its vicinity have continued to be at the heart of American Quakerism.

The Society of Friends formed a much larger fraction of the colonial population than it does of today's. The membership has scarcely doubled since 1750, while the nation has grown to thirty times the numbers it had when Washington was inaugurated as the first President. Part of the reason for the slow growth of Quakerism, even under conditions of full religious freedom, is that immigrants to America brought their own miscellaneous religious traditions with them, and maintained those traditions here through their children as well as for themselves. Indeed, the very tolerance of the Quakers contributed largely to this end. Coming to Pennsylvania at Penn's own invitation, German Lutherans and pietists, and Scotch-Irish Presbyterians, soon greatly outnumbered their Quaker precursors and hosts.

The other part of the reason for the lack of numbers in the Society is that being a Friend is a very difficult affair. There were to begin with the external marks, on which George Fox had laid very great stress: more stress than many modern Friends think was necessary or wise. The Quakers wore a plain and uniform garb, and the men kept their hats on as a defiance of fashionable, formal servility. They would not swear to an oath, and so for long were at grave disadvantage in court procedures. They refused to use the second person plural in addressing an individual, and so were marked as peculiar in their habits of speech.

They were opposed to war, therefore of course to military service, and were subject ever and again to the charge of disloyalty. Holding that the names of the days and months were of pagan origin, and that the traditional Church festivals were no less pagan, they scarcely could use the same calendar as did their neighbors. Repudiating both Baptism and the Communion as empty formalities, they scandalized people who attached special and often supernatural value to these observances. All these things made the Friends visibly different; and since most men and women are deeply afraid of being different, most people not brought up in Quaker families preferred to stay where they were.

Much more difficult, in reality, were the less visible demands of the Quakers' way of life. Solitude and silence frighten us, and we take refuge in crowds and noise. Absolute honesty is a heavy demand which deep in ourselves we are reluctant to meet. The way of personal mystic experience is one few of us learn to tread. The symbols we have derived from our heritage are dear to us, and we are unwilling to surrender them. Most of us admire the Quakers tremendously, for their life compels our admiration. Few of us think seriously of becoming Quakers ourselves.

When the 'Children of Light' realized that they had become the 'Society of Friends,' they had begun to face the perplexing and still unresolved question which the nature of their faith poses to them. They were individualists of the first water, and they insisted that only personal attitude and personal illumination mattered. At the same time they were a group. As a group they were forced to adopt uniform standards and procedures, to set up criteria by which membership might be recognized. As a matter of fact the Quakers have been a much more cohesive group than have the Congregationalists, and in many ways they have exercised as strict an internal discipline as has any branch of the Christian movement at any time in history.

Rejecting the current symbols of secular society and of the Churches, in language and calendar and clothes and modes of worship, the Quakers inescapably created a new and scarcely less rigid symbolism of their own. One day in Palestine the writer was talking with a distinguished Arab Friend, and was expressing his admiration for what the Friends had done in social service, in contending against the war spirit, in practising good will toward all men. 'If you feel that way,' the Quaker said, 'why don't you join us?' 'I might,' was the reply, 'only I don't happen to like your ritual.' He waited a moment, then nodded his head. 'Yes. I see what you mean.'

The ritual of the silent meeting of course has been modified with the course of time. In that same Quaker mission in Palestine the Wednesday evening service was a genuine silent meeting, quite unprogrammed and sometimes completely without sound. (At other times, it must be confessed, the 'spirit moved' some of the members to rather extraordinary utterances in realms not recognizably religious.) But the Sunday morning service, at which some two hundred boys and girls from the Mission boarding schools were present by requirement, did not lend itself to this usage. It differed from an ordinary Protestant Church service only in that there were pauses between the various parts.

Under pressure of neighborly example, Friends in the American Midwest have moved far from the silent meeting and from the denial of ministerial leadership. There are 'Friends' Churches' which scarcely differ from any other Protestant Church of the familiar midwestern type, and which have regular 'pastors' so titled. In Berkeley, California, are a 'Friends' Meeting House' and a 'First Friends' Church,' their buildings scarcely more than a mile apart, which have little in common as to either customs of worship or formal organization. They belong to two different and quite independent overhead associations; and while the 'Friends' Meeting' follows strictly the pattern of silent worship, the 'Friends' Church' conducts programmed services with the sermon topics announced in advance.

The same sort of contradiction in logic exists in the much more important question of the Friends' attitude toward war. On the one hand, the individual's conscience is held to be the absolute determinant of his action. On the other, there is the strong tradition of the Quaker 'witness' against war at all times and under any conditions. It may be that there was some confusion at this point from the very beginning, for George Fox seems to have supported Cromwell's war with the Dutch, and to have become clearly pacifist only with the accession of Charles II.

In practice the Friends of today differ only relatively, on the war question, from other modern Protestant groups. Most of their young men have been willing, in the two German wars, to engage in noncombatant military duties: ambulance service and the like. Some have gone further, seeing these conflicts as of such compelling moral importance as to justify their full military participation. Others have maintained the old position in full strictness, refusing even noncombatant service. These last again are divided among themselves, between those who have registered for the draft and accepted assignment to the Civilian Public Service camps for conscientious objectors, and those who refuse even to register and therefore go willingly to prison.

Of seven thousand men at present in the 'C.O.' camps, only a few over three hundred are Quakers. A larger number are Methodists, though these constitute a smaller proportion of their Church of six million members. Actually the largest group in the camps is that of the Mennonites, who have held to their pacifist views with far greater persistency than have the majority of the Friends.

As an earnest and thoughtful Quaker recently observed, 'The difficulty with us is that we're half anarchists and half socialists.' That puts it quite accurately: and perhaps for others as truly as for members of the Society of Friends. It is the old problem of freedom and order, of individual choice and social obligation. The Friends have not quite solved the problem, as their several splits and their frequent controversies have shown; and none of the rest of us have solved it either.

It is easy thus to criticize Quakerism as it has developed during the centuries. Its basic theory of individual insight makes the logical problem more apparent and more difficult than do the positions either of the Catholic or of the Congregational type of Christianity, with their dependence respectively on central authority and on majority votes. The fact remains that the Friends have been and are a vital force in our society as a whole, and that they continue to do much that compels our respect and calls for our imitation.

Almost first among Americans, the Quakers saw the wrongness of human slavery and spoke out about it. John Woolman, whose brave and tender spirit shines out from every page of his *Journal*, insisted that 'Liberty is the natural Right of all men equally,' and campaigned continually against the slave trade and slave ownership. The Friends' Meetings took stronger and stronger action against the owning of slaves by their members, and by the close of the eighteenth century had a settled policy of expelling all slaveholders from their ranks. That they did this in the South as well as in the North is the strongest witness to their sincerity; the Methodists, the Presbyterians, and the Baptists did not do so well, their Southern members finding their consciences somehow able to operate along the same lines as their supposed economic interests.

The Quakers have maintained their concern for minority groups through the years since legal slavery came to an end. Woolman was one of the first to be concerned about the unhappy status of the 'free' laborer, on the land and at sea. In 1869 President Grant turned over to the Friends the administration of Indian problems in this country; and the Friends did their work faithfully and wisely. In recent years they have been in the forefront in seeking to lessen racial antagonisms and to promote mutual understanding. It is a striking symbol, and one wholly relevant, that the present headquarters of the American Friends' Service Committee in San Francisco are in the heart of what was formerly the Japanese section of the city, now very definitely a Negro settlement.

For a generation this American Friends' Service Committee has helped to bind up the wounds of a suffering humanity in places and at times which were impossible for any other agency. It may have been a bit naïve to talk about 'loving Hitler into the Kingdom of God.' Nevertheless this naïve sort of love made possible Quaker activity in Germany, in service to needy human beings regardless of their politics, when almost no other non-Nazi agency could do anything at all. This naïve sort of love went into Europe during and after the First German War, and administered huge funds without prejudice and without criticism. This naïve sort of love has forced the whole Christian Church to rethink its values, to seek more urgently for a Christian solution to the problems of human conflict.

A word should be said too about the practice of silence. It is not for all of us a favorite way of public worship, since some of us have found the words and symbols of the historic Church to be active and vital means of grace. Many of us personally do not like a ritual which seems to us sparse and barren and unlovely. Yet the Quaker poses to all of us, in and from his silence, a very direct question as to whether our words and our other symbols really serve us as means to the end of religious illumination and experience.

No candles flicker in the Quaker sanctuary. When the candles are lit in others, do they do for us anything as to the lighting of our spirits? The Friends seldom use the Lord's Prayer. When we say it, do we really pray or do we engage in 'vain repetitions'? Participants in the silent meeting wear their ordinary clothes. When the cleric wears robes, is he accepting and transmitting a meaningful tradition, or merely fitting better into a color scheme? There is no crucifix in the meeting house. When we see the crucifix in one of the more ornate sanctuaries, do we see the gift of sacrificial love that was given on the Cross of Calvary?

It may be healthy for us sometimes to try to get along without the symbols. Perhaps our missing them will help us another time to appreciate them the more, to use them the better. Perhaps the challenge of the silence will frighten us a little: will frighten us into more honest examination of our own spirits. 'Be still, and know that I am God.' Can we know God in the stillness? If we cannot, it may be that it is not a very real God whom we know in words spoken or sung. 'Believe on the light, that ye may be children of the light.' The light's shining means little to us, does little for us, unless and until it shines within.

'In this Silence we learn abiding in the Divine will.' In this silence, unrelieved by decoration or by dramatic movement; in the silence of our own spirits, consciously sought and bravely faced wherever we may be; in the light that shines within us, whatever the outer darkness: can we learn? can we find? If we can, then we can live as Children of the Light.

X

'IS THY HEART RIGHT?'

(The Methodists)

'Is thine heart right, as my heart is with thy heart? . . . If it be, give me thine hand.'—II Kings 10:15 (AV); used by John Wesley as the text of his sermon on 'Catholic Spirit.'

'Rejoice in the Lord alway.'—Philippians 4:4 (AV).

'I felt my heart strangely warmed.'
        —John Wesley, *Journal*, 24 May 1738.

'I look upon all the world as my parish.'—John Wesley to the Bishop of London, 11 May 1739.

'Scream no more, at the peril of your soul.'—John Wesley, letter to a lay preacher.

'I declare, once more, that I live and die a member of the Church of England, and that none who regard my judgment will ever separate from it.'—John Wesley, farewell letter to the Methodist societies, 1790.

OFTEN it may be noted, in books on Comparative Religion or about the various branches of Christianity, that the author has carefully reserved his own tradition to discuss last, so that he may set it forth as being the best of all. Since the present writer happens to be a Methodist, he may be suspected of having done just that in his arranging of these studies of the Protestant Churches within the total Hebrew-Christian tradition. We have looked at Lutheranism and Presbyterianism and Anglicanism, at the Congregationalists and the Baptists and the Quakers. Now we come to Methodism, with only the Disciples remaining to be considered among the denominational groups. Has the writer loaded the dice?

He pleads 'not guilty.' The order throughout has been simply chronological, from Luther's nailing up of his ninety-five theses in 1517 to George Fox's vision of 'an ocean of light and love' in 1646. Here we move up ninety-two years more, to the 'strange warming' of Wesley's heart at a little meeting on Aldersgate Street, in London, on 24 May 1738. History, and not personal preference, determined the sequence of chapters; and that Methodism is the second youngest of the Protestant traditions we are considering in detail may be its good fortune but is not necessarily its merit.

John Wesley was born in 1703, the fifteenth of nineteen children of the Reverend and Mrs. Samuel Wesley of the parish of Epworth in Lincolnshire. His father, brought up as a Dissenter, had worked his way through Oxford and had taken orders in the established Church. John's mother, Susannah, was the stronger of the parents, and was counsellor and guide to her strongest son throughout the long years that she continued to live. A younger brother, Charles (the eighteenth child in the family, and four years junior to John), is the other Wesley of whom we must take special account.

The brothers went to two different prep schools, but came together again at Christ Church College, Oxford. As a seat of learning Oxford in the eighteenth century left much to be desired. Said the historian Gibbon of the dons of his time, forty years after Wesley's:

From the toil of reading, or thinking, or writing, they had absolved their conscience. . . . Their conversation stagnated in a round of college business, Tory politics, personal anecdotes, and private scandal.

(It sounds as though some of us modern academicians might have felt quite at home!)

But it is possible, even despite an indifferent faculty, for a student to do serious work if he is determined to; and this kind of determination the Wesleys had. In 1725 John Wesley read eagerly the monastic Thomas à Kempis' *Imitation of Christ* and the High Church Bishop Jeremy Taylor's *Holy Living and Dying*, and decided to become a candidate for ordination. He made out for himself a set of detailed rules of intention and behavior, and started a shorthand diary which he kept up for sixty-five years thereafter.

When Charles came up to Oxford, he gathered about him a little company of students who believed, as did the Wesleys, in the unusual and unpopular practices of studying, of obeying University rules, and of taking Holy Communion regularly. Naturally these rare birds attracted notice, and some wag remarked, 'Here is a new set of method-ists sprung up!' John was away at the time, serving as assistant to his father in Epworth Church; but he came back in 1729 as a Fellow of Lincoln College, was gladly welcomed into the informal society, and quickly became its real leader. Other names were attached to the group: 'Sacramentarians,' 'Bible Moths,' 'Holy Club.' But 'Method-ists' stuck and gained currency, and the methodical young men came to accept the term as the Friends had the label of 'Quakers.'

In 1735 the two Wesley brothers, eager to carry the gospel to the 'noble savages' of the New World, went as missionaries to General Oglethorpe's recently founded colony of Georgia. Aboard the same ship was a party of German Moravians, whose forerunners had broken from Rome fifty years before Luther. A great storm frightened John Wesley badly, and then made him ashamed when he heard the Moravians calmly singing a psalm. He never forgot that, and after landing continued to ask for guidance from the Moravian leaders.

The Georgia venture was a failure. The Indians showed no eagerness to be converted, and ere long John Wesley decided that they were less 'noble' than he had supposed. Moreover he got involved in a love affair which he handled with inordinate stuffiness. (One sample will suffice: He took the girl boating, and spent the afternoon reading to her from Fleury's *History of the Church;* after which he proposed, got an uncertain answer, and, says his diary, 'We ended the conversation with a Psalm.') More to his credit, he got into trouble with the colonists by fearlessly opposing slavery. Finally a Grand Jury indicted him for various ecclesiastical offences, including attempts to inflict penances and to require confession of those who wished to take Holy Communion.

The case was complicated by the personal involvement of the young lady, and by bitter opposition to Wesley on the part of her relatives. It never came to trial. Wesley returned to London, bewildered and broken-hearted. There he once more sought out the Moravians, especially one Peter Böhler, a graduate of the University of Jena and a pronounced mystic. Little by little Wesley came to grasp the meaning of personal faith as the inward power of life. He began to preach in these terms; and then came 24 May 1738. Wesley had attended the afternoon service at St. Paul's Cathedral, and had listened earnestly to the Choir's chanting of the 130th Psalm, the *De Profundis:* 'Out of the depths have I cried unto thee, O Lord.' Then, says his *Journal:*

In the evening I went very unwillingly to a society in Aldersgate Street where one was reading Luther's preface to the Epistle to the Romans. About a quarter before nine, while he was describing the change which God works in the heart through faith in Christ, I felt my heart strangely warmed. I felt I did trust in Christ, Christ alone for my salvation; and an assurance was given me that he had taken away my sins, even mine, and saved me from the law of sin and death.

There has been among later Methodists a popular myth to the effect that this 'conversion' turned John Wesley into something wholly different from what he was before, particularly that it made him reject all his former High Church views to the point of actively fighting against them. The evidence argues otherwise. Wesley continued to practise and to urge daily private acts of devotion and weekly receiving of the Holy Communion. He nowhere clearly asserts, but he never bothered to attack, his brother Charles' unquestionable belief in the 'real presence' of the body and blood of Christ in the Communion elements. He relaxed not at all his intense devotion to the Church as an institution. He had not changed his religion. He had found new vitality in it, and in himself.

He was much too vital for the Church of his own time.

Puritanism had made the services dull and unlovely. Ignorance and idleness had made preaching infrequent and unhelpful. Self-satisfaction had made dominant English society wholly indifferent both to the physical and to the spiritual health of the people. Wesley wanted true services of worship, faithfully conducted according to the rules laid down. He wanted to preach, thoughtfully and powerfully. He wanted to reach the people: and the people were not in the Churches, and would not have been very welcome had they come.

By 1739 there were only three or four London Churches that would let this eager and upsetting young man conduct services in them. In that year George Whitefield, who had followed Wesley to Georgia and who unlike Wesley had become very popular there, returned to England. Whitefield, finding himself also excluded from the regular pulpits, decided to preach out of doors to the coal-miners at Kingswood Colliery near Bristol: to men who had no Church they could well attend. Wesley at first was shocked, then was greatly impressed by Whitefield's success. On 2 April 1739 he preached his own first outdoor sermon: on the text, 'The Spirit of the Lord is upon me, because he hath anointed me to preach the Gospel to the poor.'

Thus, mostly out of doors and chiefly to the poor, he preached for fifty-one more years. He rode, with his sermons in his saddle-bags and in his heart, two hundred fifty thousand miles through English weather and over eighteenth-century roads. Estimates of the number of sermons he preached from 1738 to 1791 vary from 40,000 to 52,400. In his *Journal* for eight consecutive days in May of 1784, when he was eighty-one years old, may be counted thirteen sermons preached in seven different towns in the far north of Scotland. His last sermon was in London eight days before he died, at the age of eighty-eight. Only four days before his death he wrote to William Wilberforce, the great opponent of slavery, congratulating him on his

glorious enterprise in opposing that execrable villainy which is the scandal of religion, of England, and of human nature . . . Go on [he added] in the name of God, and in the power of His might, till even American slavery (the vilest that ever saw the sun) shall vanish before it.

Long before these last days, Wesley had to face the same result of his preaching as had confronted the Independents and the Quakers: the problem of organization and discipline for those who had found a new expression of their own religious faith. Wesley had no idea of setting up a new nonconformist denomination. He organized his adherents into local 'societies,' instructing them to remain faithful in attendance at the Church of England in their own parishes, and to partake often of the Communion. The 'societies' thus were created as fellowships within the Church, not at all as an independent community apart from it. Over each local group Wesley set a 'class leader,' whom he held responsible for the spiritual welfare and personal conduct of all the members. Because few of the regular clergy would work with Wesley at all, he reluctantly instituted a system of lay preaching. For these volunteer workers he set up and enforced high standards of moral and intellectual qualification, but we find him often complaining of the difficulties he had in holding them in line.

Methodism quickly made its way to America, and now with a success that Wesley himself never had known in

Georgia. When the Revolution came a new set of problems appeared. The Bishops and clergy of the Church of England in the Colonies, as we noted previously, as officials of the Crown naturally were Tories; and almost all of them fled or were driven out. Wesley himself was no radical in politics, and had written two pamphlets in opposition to the Colonial point of view. But with the breakdown of Anglicanism a new situation existed, in which there was no one to administer the Sacraments or to guide the affairs of the Church. Wesley, whose last thought was to establish a new denomination in England, found himself impelled to create a new Church in the United States.

Let him tell the story himself, in the certificate he issued to Dr. Thomas Coke on 2 September 1784:

Whereas many of the people of the Southern provinces of North America, who desire to continue under my care, and still adhere to the doctrine and discipline of the Church of England, are greatly distressed for want of ministers to administer the sacraments of baptism and the Lord's supper, according to the usages of the same church: and whereas there does not appear to be any other way of supplying them with ministers:

Know all men, that I, John Wesley, think myself to be providentially called at this time to set apart some persons for the work of the ministry in America. And, therefore, under the protection of Almighty God, and with a single eye to His glory, I have this day set apart as a Superintendent, by the imposition of my hands, and prayer, (being assisted by other ordained ministers,) Thomas Coke, Doctor of Civil Law, a Presbyter of the Church of England, and a man whom I judge to be well qualified for that great work. And I do hereby recommend him to all whom it may concern, as a fit person to preside over the flock of Christ.

Arriving in New York, Dr. Coke led a conference which organized itself into the Methodist Episcopal Church in the United States of America. Francis Asbury, a lay preacher, was elected a second Superintendent, and on three successive days was ordained deacon and elder, and consecrated to the Superintendency. Wesley had avoided the use of the word 'Bishop,' but from the beginning the American Church employed it: on the interesting ground that the New Testament referred to 'Bishops,' but had nothing to say about 'Superintendents.' The Constitution of the Methodist Episcopal Church, prior to the recent union of the American Methodist groups, called the highest officers 'General Superintendents,' though the legislation enacted under that Constitution mentioned them consistently as 'Bishops.' In the Constitution of the newly united Church the 'Bishops' appear as such without apology and without embarrassment.

For the new Church in America Wesley arranged also

a liturgy, little differing from that of the Church of England (I think the best constituted national church in the world), which I advise all the travelling preachers to use on the Lord's day in all congregations . . . I also advise the elders to administer the Supper of the Lord on every Lord's day.

Wesley also arranged an abridgement of the Psalms for responsive reading, leaving out some imprecations which, he said, were 'not fit to be in a Christian's mouth.' The 'Wesley Sunday Service' follows closely the Anglican pattern of Morning Prayer. The Methodist Communion Service also is practically identical with that of the Episcopal Churches, as are the forms for Baptism, Marriage, Ordination, and Burial. In the present official *Methodist Hymnal* is the music of a complete Choral Communion, along with numerous settings for the traditional chants of Morning and Evening Prayer. The full Sunday Service long was practically ignored in American Methodism, but it is being increasingly adopted in our time.

Methodist enthusiasm carried the movement far and fast. As it spread from the seaboard across the Alleghenies and through the Cumberland Gap it was influenced by other religious traditions, and also by the conditions of pioneer life. Wesley himself always had been strongly opposed to the sale and use of intoxicants, because he had seen their calamitous effect on the English people to whom he ministered. Other aspects of Puritanism found their way into Methodist values in America, until the Methodist Church perhaps more than others came to be identified with rigid rules against not only drinking, but also dancing, smoking, card-playing and theatre-going. These latter have not been understood by English Methodists to constitute moral questions, and they are less and less emphasized by American Methodists today. As time went on frontier Methodism more than ever lost touch with the Anglican tradition, for the Protestant Episcopal Church long stayed close to the eastern seaboard; and so more and more Methodist services in America were pulled toward the informal type of the Puritans and other dissenting sects.

By its nature highly missionary in spirit, Methodism has spread throughout the world. The number of communicant members is about twelve million, with perhaps a total of thirty million more or less closely affiliated adherents. The recent union of the Churches North and South, and with them of the Methodist Protestant Church, has brought together more than six million Church members into the largest single Protestant unit in this country. English Methodism, led by the lay preachers who wanted full clerical status for themselves and were denied it by the incumbent Bishops, rejected Wesley's injunction to remain within the established Church. Soon after his death, following the American example, they set up a separate (but non-episcopal) Church in Great Britain. There followed numerous subdividings on issues more or less important; but in this century successive reunions have created a single English Methodist Church of approximately a million members.

John Wesley never was interested primarily in theological questions, and here the Methodist Churches have followed his lead. Attempts to establish sharp doctrinal tests for membership or ordination have been consistently defeated, often by direct reference to Wesley's famous 'Catholic Spirit' sermon, in which he urged that Christian unity depended on uniformity neither of worship nor of opinion, but only on the love of God and all mankind. 'It is certain that opinion is not religion,' he insisted; 'not even right opinion.' From the Thirty-Nine Articles of Religion of the Church of England Wesley selected twenty-four that he thought important, and added to them one recognizing the government of the United States; but the resulting Twenty-Five Articles of Religion of the Methodist Church are quite as unfamiliar to the average Methodist as are the Thirty-Nine to the average Episcopalian.

Nevertheless there was one doctrinal point on which Wesley was very emphatic indeed, and to which he returned again and again. It was the flat denial of Calvinist determinism. Early in his career, on 29 April 1739, preaching on 'Free Grace,' he assailed the very center of Calvin's teaching:

This (he said) is the blasphemy clearly contained in the horrible decree of predestination! And here I fix my feet. On this I join issue with every asserter of it. You represent God as worse than the devil; more false, more cruel, more unjust. But you say you will prove it by Scripture? Hold! What will you prove by Scripture? That God is worse than the devil? It cannot be. Whatever that Scripture proves, it cannot prove this. . . . It cannot mean . . . that the God of truth is a liar . . . it cannot mean that the Judge of all the world is unjust. No scripture can mean that God is not love, or that his mercy is not over all his works; that is, whatever it prove beside, no scripture can prove predestination.

This thoroughgoing assertion of Free Will indeed went further than ever the official teaching of Catholicism had; but it was much nearer to the Catholic than to the Puritan view, and along with Wesley's concern for private devotion and for public worship it constitutes the evidence that the Wesleyan movement was in essence a Catholic reaction against acute Protestantism within the English Church. Both the Wesleys were commonly charged in England with being agents of the Jesuits, and in revolutionary times many Americans suspected the Methodists of being a Tory force. (Perhaps it is relevant too that Charles' son, Samuel, one of the foremost Church organists in English history, became a Catholic at eighteen and remained one all the rest of his life.) The culture of the frontier, and that of the later Midwest, greatly diluted the Catholic aspects of Methodist life and thought, until they became almost unrecognizable in the typical Methodist Church in America. Today the old emphases have been remembered and reëxamined, and they are finding their way back into Methodist attitudes and usages.

What the Methodists have kept all through, and have lived by, is Wesley's own enthusiasm, Wesley's own personal faith issuing in strenuous action. They have shouted perhaps more than he did, and more than he would have liked; but they have shouted the Gospel of God's grace and of man's freedom to accept that grace for himself. With the Wesleys they have sung their faith as have few other Christian communities. The current official *Methodist Hymnal* contains 53 hymns by Charles Wesley; but the other standard Church hymnals depend greatly on him too, as witness 18 of his hymns in the Episcopal book, 15 in the Presbyterian, and 11 in the Congregational.

Enthusiastic personal faith and eager concern for humanity have put the Methodists into the forefront of one social and moral crusade after another. The Salvation Army was founded by a member of the Methodist New Connexion, one of the smaller Methodist groups in England. In 1908 the Methodist Episcopal Church announced its 'Social Creed,' declaring for the direct application of Christian standards in economic relations; and later in the same year the Federal Council of Churches of Christ adopted that Creed practically without change. The Goodwill Industries and the Churches of All Nations, offering economic opportunity and interracial brotherhood in every major American city, both are Methodist enterprises; and both, as it happens, stem from Morgan Memorial, a Methodist Church and community center in one of the depressed sections of Boston.

As a generation ago the Methodists led the fight for

Prohibition, so in our days they have become outstanding among the larger Churches in their opposition to war. A resolution supporting the United States in the present war passed in the latest General Conference by the margin of a single vote, and the World Peace Commission of the Church has remained rather strikingly pacifist. Debates in Methodist circles occur almost invariably over such questions of action, almost never in the realm of theory.

The combination of intellectual tolerance with moral passion has made for a vigorous, growing, and changing Church. Today the Methodists perhaps are nearer to Wesley than they were in most of the years between his time and ours, for (along with many others) they have been catching up with his freedom of spirit and also have been learning something of his appreciation for the past. Asserting man's freedom to find rich, abundant personal life, and with it man's obligation to serve the welfare of every other human life, Methodism has the kind of message that is newly appropriate in each new set of circumstances. Organized closely and authoritatively, yet hospitable to differences both within and outside the fellowship, Methodism has the kind of structure that makes a Church both free and orderly.

Some of us are convinced that it yielded too much, especially in the American scene, to the spirit of negative dissent and of Puritan rigidity. It lost a great deal when it forgot Wesley's valuation of worship, and when it abandoned his practice of frequent Communion. It is to be doubted whether the Methodist Churches would satisfy Mr. Wesley, even today, in the details of their procedure. But Wesley was too powerful a force ever to be written off the record, even when special pleading obscured the real emphases of his teaching and life; and in the warm heart and the friendly hand the Methodists have been true to the central and the best in Wesley's mission.

'Rejoice in the Lord alway.' 'The world is my parish.' 'Is thine heart right, as my heart is with thy heart? If it be, then give me thine hand.' Joy; eagerness; friendliness: these are fruits of the Spirit of Christ. As fruits of the spirit of Methodism they are of the essence of the Christian life.

XI

'WHERE THE SCRIPTURES SPEAK'

(The Disciples of Christ)

*'Every one of you saith, I am of Paul; and I of Apollos; and
I of Cephas; and I of Christ. Is Christ divided?'*
—I Corinthians 1:12f (AV).

*'All scripture is given by inspiration of God, and is profit-
able for doctrine, for reproof, for correction, for in-
struction in righteousness.'*—II Timothy 3:16 (AV).

*'Where the Scriptures speak, we speak; and where the
Scriptures are silent, we are silent.'*—Thomas Camp-
bell, before the Christian Association of Washington
(County), Pennsylvania, 1809.

*'We form ourselves into a religious association . . . for
the sole purpose of promoting simple, evangelical Christianity, free from all mixture of human opinions and
inventions of men. . . . This society by no means considers itself a Church.'*—From the Declaration and Address of the Christian Association of Washington,
7 September 1809.

FROM China came a young graduate student who had
grown up in a Methodist mission and had been trained in
Methodist schools. Some weeks after his arrival, a Methodist professor in the University looked him up. 'Are you
happy in your classes?' 'Yes, thank you.' 'Are you com-

fortable in your quarters?' 'Yes, thank you very much.'
And so on, until, 'Have you found a Church to attend?'
'Oh yes, thank you; I go to the First Church.' 'Oh, of
course: at 6th and Q Streets.' 'No: at 9th and Y.' 'Oh, the
First *Christian* Church!' 'But certainly, the Christian
Church: I am a Christian.'

The Methodist missionaries who brought up that boy
did well to impress on him that he was a Christian more
than he was a Methodist. And the boy did naturally
enough in asking, on his first Sunday in a new land, for
directions to 'a Christian Church.' But neither the missionaries nor he had thought of 'Christian' as a term of denominational separation. No more did Alexander Campbell intend that it should be: yet it was largely through
his activities that it became so.

The story begins with Alexander's father, Thomas, an
'Anti-Burgher' Presbyterian minister in Northern Ireland,
who in 1807 was advised to take a sea voyage for his health.
Thomas Campbell's first letter from Philadelphia, to the
family he had left in County Armagh, expressed his intention to settle in the new country and to send for them. He
found his way to Washington County, Pennsylvania, and
became minister of the Seceder Presbyterian Church in a
Scotch-Irish settlement. Experience with the numerous di-
vidings of Presbyterianism, and with the innumerable sects
appearing and developing in the American scene, turned
Campbell's mind to the need for true Christian union. He
began to welcome outsiders to the Communion, and for
this unorthodox behavior was condemned by his Presbytery.

Though on appeal he was formally upheld by the Synod,

which seems to have been impressed by Campbell's argument that the Bible said nothing about 'closed communion,' he found the atmosphere unfriendly. In 1809 he and his followers withdrew and formed 'The Christian Association of Washington.' This definitely was not intended to be a new Church, much less a new denomination, but rather a fellowship open to all Christians and a renewal of New Testament Christianity. Its *Declaration and Address*, written by Campbell, was a plea for Christian union on the basis of New Testament simplicity.

Our differences, at most, (the *Declaration* urges) are about matters in which the Kingdom of God does not consist; that is, about matters of private opinion or human invention. What a pity that the kingdom of God should be divided about such things! . . . There is nothing we have hitherto received as matter of faith or practice which is not expressly taught and enjoined in the Word of God, either in express terms or approved precedent, that we would not heartily relinquish, that so we might return to the original constitutional unity of the Christian Church, and in this happy unity enjoy full communion with all our brethren in peace and charity. . . . Nothing ought to be received into the faith or worship of the Church, or be made a term of communion among Christians, that is not as old as the New Testament.

Two years later, meeting continued Presbyterian frost, and feeling the need of regularizing its own procedure, the Association organized itself as a new 'First Church.' Alexander, now twenty-one years old, was licensed as a preacher. Studying the New Testament in order to identify the minimum Christian essentials, Alexander Campbell concluded in favor of weekly administration of the

Lord's Supper, believer's baptism, and immersion, as being the symbols authoritatively enjoined and therefore binding. The two points about baptism brought the 'Campbellites' (as now their neighbors called them) very close indeed to the Baptists. In 1812 they were invited to join the Redstone Baptist Association, and willingly accepted.

This phase of unity lasted almost twenty years, but it was one of increasingly uneasy fellowship. Campbell seemed to the Baptists unduly keen on the importance of the New Testament, to the disparagement of the Old. He was essentially a voluntarist, whereas most of the Baptists still held to Calvinistic assumptions. He questioned whether an ordained ministry were permissible, an attitude which did not endear him to his ordained Baptist brothers. He was willing to receive members on their own profession of Christian faith, while Baptist custom provided for congregational scrutiny and congregational vote. (That difference between Baptists and Disciples persists even until now.) Though Campbell insisted on a weekly Communion service, he was rather casual as to the way in which it should be conducted.

In July of 1830 Alexander Campbell suspended publication of his magazine, *The Christian Baptist*, which he had founded in 1823. In the final editorial he observed:

I have commenced a new work, and taken a new name for it on various accounts. Hating sects and sectarian names, I resolved to prevent the name of Christian Baptists from being fixed upon us, to do which efforts were making. It is true, men's tongues are their own, and they may use them as they please; but I am resolved to give them no just occasion for nicknaming advocates for the ancient order of things.

The 'new work' was *The Millennial Harbinger*, which Campbell continued to edit until early in 1865, and to which he contributed until a few months before his death in 1866.

All in all, 'Campbellite' independency was too supple to stay within the rapidly crystallizing Baptist pattern. Doctrinal controversies arose over the intention of the sacraments, the way in which the Holy Spirit operated in salvation, and (underlying these) the effective freedom of human decision. In the spring of 1830 the Third Baptist Church of Philadelphia excluded a number of Campbell's followers, who promptly organized themselves into an independent Church. Conservative Baptists in Kentucky assailed the 'Campbellites,' and the Elkhorn Association expelled three Churches where Campbell's views and practices prevailed. In December the Dover Association in Virginia adopted a committee report condemning the theological 'errors of Campbellism.' At Richmond the 're-formers,' asked by the Baptist pastor to withdraw, formed their own Church in March of 1832. Accepting the situation, the Campbells led their followers out of the Baptist fold. Once again the seekers of unity were a separate denomination.

They did achieve unity, almost at once, with two other like-minded fellowships. One Barton W. Stone, another ex-Presbyterian who objected to creeds and to formalism, in 1804 had organized a 'Christian Church' in Cane Ridge, Kentucky, and now was the leader of a considerable movement under that name. A similar development had occurred in Ohio under a Walter Scott. Unions with Churches of these groups began to be consummated in 1832, and were substantially complete by 1835.

The question of a name to be borne by the new body inevitably arose. The leaders agreed that only a scriptural name should be used. Campbell favored 'Disciples of Christ,' while Stone contended for 'Christian Church.' Officially Campbell won, and the technical designation remains 'Disciples of Christ.' Later usage gave the actual victory to Stone, as witness the 'First Christian Church' (of the Disciples of Christ) in city after city throughout the land. The one name that never should be used, because the denomination objects to it, is 'Disciples' Church.' The spiritual children of Alexander Campbell are the 'Disciples of Christ,' and constitute the 'Christian Churches' of their respective communities.

The simple, Biblical teaching of the Disciples, and their avoidance of all rigid forms, gave the newly united fellowship a great appeal to the simple, informal, Bible-believing people of the West. Stressing the rights of individual conscience, the Disciples avoided any open break on the slavery question; Campbell himself opposed slavery, but sought for its gradual abolition by democratic, legal process. By the beginning of the War of 1861–65 the Disciples counted two hundred thousand members. Growth continued, chiefly in the Midwest, and the million mark was reached about the beginning of this century. As was noted above, this makes the Disciples the second largest group in this country holding to the congregational form of organization.

It is *the* American Christian group, the only major denomination sprung from the American soil, and the most completely American in its character. It is indebted directly to the Presbyterians and the Baptists, directly also to the New Testament. It is indebted no less to the frontier which created it, and which in turn it helped to mold. Its major innovation among Protestant fellowships, and the one feature that makes its regular Sunday services unmistakably different from those of other nonconformist groups, was the institution of the weekly Lord's Supper. This indeed was a return to the past, coming close to Catholic and Anglican tradition, and to John Wesley's preference; but the administration was and still is after the frontier fashion, informal and with laymen taking leading parts. Whether or not the Christian Churches become the matrix of a newly united Christian Church, they are already a union of all the elements and all the forces that have made American Christianity what it is.

Alexander Campbell soon found himself confronted, as had so many before him, by the antinomy between freedom and order. Decisive and methodical in his own mind, he swung (again as did many decisive leaders before him) more and more toward order. Not only did he organize the American Christian Missionary Society, but also he founded Bethany College in West Virginia and became its President. Both for missions and for education he had to raise money, and so for both he had to establish boards and to delegate authority. Before his death the Disciples were a full-fledged denomination with all the paraphernalia and all the problems of a complex denominational structure.

The moral seems to be that union is not so simple as it sounds. Even in Corinth, as St. Paul indicates, sectarianism quickly developed; and already there 'of Christ' had become a term of separation rather than one of inclusion. Take, for example, the principle of 'where the Scriptures speak.' Yes: but just what do they say? Campbell could not persuade the Calvinists that the Bible taught voluntarism, the Methodists that it demanded believer's baptism by immersion, the Baptists that it required weekly communion. Nor did he realize fully the further complications to be introduced by the rise of Biblical criticism and the reëstimating of the nature of scriptural authority.

Yet Alexander Campbell was far ahead of his time in his freedom from slavish dependence upon a single English rendering. One of his notable enterprises, even though now a forgotten one, was a 'New Version' of the New Testament, issued in 1827. It was compiled largely from the exegetical works of George Campbell, Macknight, and Doddridge, and moved far toward simplification and the use of the American vernacular. With it he published the important and too little known preface of the 'Translators to the Reader,' from the version of 1611. Writing in the final number of *The Christian Baptist*, 4 July 1830, in reply to an attack upon his own venture, Alexander Campbell declared:

I am always prepared to defend not only the New Version which I have published, but the necessity of new versions for the confirmation of the faith and the enlargement of the views of christians.

Campbell's substituting, for the Greek-English 'baptize,' of the Latin-English 'immerse' (he went not so far as the literal Anglo-Saxon 'dip'), of course made his translation unacceptable to most of the Churches; and the conservatism of his own followers, disposed to recognize only the 1611 version as being 'The Bible,' soon relegated this daring innovation to obscurity.

So far from uniting the Disciples with others, the canon of dependence on the Bible has served to divide the Disciples themselves. Some of them have journeyed with Campbell in maintaining active intellectual enquiry; others have preferred to stay with him in the knowledge and opinions he reached in his own time. Early in this century one conservative group of 'Churches of Christ' broke away, and remain apart with more than three hundred thousand members. In 1931 those who traced their heritage specifically to Barton W. Stone, constituting the 'General Convention of the Christian Church,' and numbering something over one hundred thousand, united with the Congregationalists.

There remain two organizationally connected but quite distinct 'wings' of the Disciples, not moving at all in unison. The right wing continues to be literalist, revivalist, individualist. The other is not merely the left wing of the 'Christian Churches,' but is wellnigh the left wing-tip of American Protestantism.

Under the long and distinguished editorship of Charles Clayton Morrison, the organ of this party, *The Christian Century*, has become the standard weekly journal of all liberal Christians in the United States, of whatever denomination. There are among its readers, for example, many more Methodists than there are Disciples; and Dr. Morrison's able associate, Paul Hutchinson, was brought to the paper in (not out of) the Methodist Church. The *Century* takes Biblical criticism for granted, ignores the supernaturalistic millennial hope, characteristically supports organized labor against employers, and for long was stringently pacifist in tone. In detail it may seem a strange successor to *The Christian Baptist* and *The Millennial Harbinger;* yet in independence of spirit and frankness of utterance it is fully within the Campbell tradition.

In general the lines of demarcation among the Disciples follow the cultural patterns of the country. Conservative attitudes prevail in the agricultural regions, in the small towns, and in most of the smaller Churches. Liberal preaching characterizes many of the pulpits in metropolitan areas, and becomes increasingly prevalent as young ministers come to the Christian Churches from (once Presbyterian) Union, and (once Baptist) Chicago, and (once Congregational) Pacific School of Religion: schools to which most of the young men have gone with the full approval of their own denomination.

The Disciples, or at all events the liberals in their ranks, continue to be leaders in the cause of Christian union. *The Christian Century* is an active distributor of common information, and a powerful agent toward unity of opinion and feeling, among liberal Christians of all the Churches. In 1910 the National Convention, recalling the 'Christian Association' of a hundred years before, organized its new 'Association for the Promotion of Christian Unity,' which still operates as one of the official agencies of the denomination. Peter Ainslie of the Christian Temple in Baltimore, one of the outstanding ministers of the Disciples in our time, created the interdenominational and international Christian Unity League for Equality and Brotherhood, and for many years proclaimed Alexander Campbell's message in modern terms through his ably edited *Christian Union Quarterly*, which in 1935 was absorbed into the ecumenical *Christendom*.

Immediately, the effective unification most likely to take place is that of the Disciples with the Baptists. These two groups have at least as much in common as they did when they came together in 1812: believer's baptism, immersion, congregational autonomy; and they now have much less of minor, technical controversy with which to reckon than they did in 1832. One problem remaining is that of the congregational vote on new members, another that of the weekly communion. A minister of a Christian Church tells the writer he believes the liberal Baptists are willing to give up the voting point, the liberal Disciples the sacramental. Another possibility is that on both matters the rule of congregational preference might be allowed to prevail.

The name is another question. Would the Baptists willingly give up a title honored in three centuries of consecrated heroism? Would the Disciples accept a 'sectarian' and non-Biblical designation? And what would the Methodists, the Presbyterians, and the Anglicans think of a denomination not of one million members, but of almost nine million, taking to itself the name 'Christian' as a special distinguishing mark?

Fortunately it is not the name that matters, either for the Christian Churches (Disciples of Christ) or for the Christian Church. Perhaps Alexander Campbell was right after all. Perhaps unity, which is more important than union, is available if we agree upon simplicity and reduce our stress upon disagreements. Whether we renounce creeds, or reinterpret them; whether we say the Bible is not finally authoritative, or admit that its authority may be understood in different ways; whether we diversify baptism or open the communion: we shall find that there are lowest common denominators which may become highest, and very high, common factors.

'All scripture is given by inspiration of God.' The Greek has a larger meaning in our own day, a meaning perhaps larger than was intended by the early Christian commentator who added that remark to St. Paul's note to the young Timothy. 'Every God-inspired writing,' we would render it if we knew no other version, 'is profitable for teaching.' And among the God-inspired, profitable writings we readily may include, along with Luther's *Table Talk* and Calvin's *Institutes* and Wesley's *Sermons*, the Washington County *Declaration and Address*. There is inspiration here. The proof is that it has inspired faith, and activity, and fullness of religious experience. This is part of the Scriptures that speak to us, and much of this part we shall do well to echo.

Specifically, the Disciples and the Baptists will not come together with the other Churches so long as they insist upon believer's baptism only and upon immersion only. Specifically, congregational independence will not soon be assimilated to episcopal leadership. It was, after all, because the Campbells were a little too specific that their dream of union remained unrealized, that their projected association of all Christians became yet another Christian sect. History has proved that the Campbells had not discovered all the right answers. It still is possible that they asked the right questions. 'Is Christ divided?' Why?

XII

'TEST ALL THINGS'

(The Liberal Christians)

'Test all things: hold fast the good.'
— I Thessalonians 5:21 (GH).

'Ye shall know the truth, and the truth shall make you free.'
— St. John 8:32 (AV).

AT THIS point, much more than has been the case hitherto, our problem is one of definition. We have sought to describe and to evaluate, in turn, the Jewish, the Orthodox, the Catholic, and the various Protestant elements in our common religious culture. In each of the preceding cases we could start with a specific, identifiable group and a recognizable complex of attitudes. Liberalism, however, and perhaps by its very nature, is vague as a concept and scarcely existent as a structure. Nevertheless it is a reality within the pattern of American Christianity, and because it can be identified with no single Church it must here be studied in its own right.

At one time and another the word 'liberal' has been used to describe very nearly anything and everything. Its earlier connotation in European usage was 'generosity' almost wholly in the financial sense: thus when Machiavelli speaks of 'liberal princes' he means not 'socially conscious' monarchs but money-spending ones. In Britain the history of party politics has equated 'Liberalism' chiefly with Adam Smith economics: *laissez-faire*, free trade, the Manchester manufacturers. A few Americans still remember when in common parlance 'liberal' meant specifically 'anti-prohibitionist.' Most recently the orthodoxy of the left wing has made 'liberal' into an opprobrious epithet by absorbing it into the new and single word, 'muddledliberal.'

In the realm of religion, 'liberalism' recently has been associated with so-called 'modernism' in theology, with socialist preferences in economics, with pacifism as an international program. The kind of assumption thus made, and which constitutes the error most usually involved, was illustrated for the writer in a conversation which occurred just fourteen days before the attack on Pearl Harbor. He had been assigned the task of discussing, with a group of lay Churchmen, 'The Case for Liberal Christianity in the 1940s.' Trying to urge the necessity of continuing revision of our judgments, he mentioned the deliquescence of pacifism under the impact of recent world events. 'But,' interjected the young clergyman who had assigned the topic, 'isn't pacifism part of the content of liberal Christianity?'

The writer thought not, and thinks not: not at this point because he rejects the pacifist position *per se,* but because he denies that liberal Christianity may be identified in terms of content. Liberal Christianity, or liberalism generally, may not be defined as consisting in opinions or judgments. Liberalism as such is not conclusion, but methodology. The point of unity among liberals is one not of arrival, not even necessarily of road, but of the type of vehicle chosen for the journey.

There are modernists, and socialists, and pacifists, and men and women who are all three at once, who simply are not 'liberals' at all. *A priori* determination of theological judgment, whether it stem from Church or from Bible or from philosophical materialism: and wherever it may come out in opinion: *a priori* theology is not liberal, but strictly authoritarian. Economic dogmatism is economic dogmatism whether the dogma be phrased by Adam Smith or by Karl Marx; and the doctrinaire Socialist is just as illiberal as is the doctrinaire Republican. Sentimental pacifism is psychologically akin to sentimental patriotism; and each is equally foreign to the quality of the liberal spirit.

It is time to turn to positives. If liberalism be methodology, what methods may we identify as being proper to it? 'Liberal' connotes 'free.' The first and principal mark of true liberalism is the technique of free, objective enquiry. In our Western culture such enquiry became possible only with the Renaissance and the Reformation; and it became generally acceptable, even among scholars, only with and after the eighteenth century 'Enlightenment.' Laboratory experiment was a new device, and an unwelcome one for many specialists as well as for most laymen. Galileo was damned not only by the Church but also by his fellow-scientists. Modern academicians are familiar with what they describe as 'scientific method.' They still have to reckon with the fact that the mass of the public has not yet learned objectively to enquire, and that therefore it tends yet to distrust the findings of objective enquiry.

The application of scientific method in the field of religion has developed still more slowly, and for most religious people is as yet neither familiar nor acceptable.

Examining the Biblical records which the Protestant movement had made available, scholars began gradually to recognize that many common assumptions about the character of the Scriptures were confuted by indisputable evidence. Testing official dogma by the criteria of pure and of practical reason, thinkers found it necessary to rephrase, and sometimes to reject, formulae which previously had been accepted without criticism. In both fields Germany led the way: that Germany of science to which we owe so much, that Germany born free which now we hope shall escape altogether from its erstwhile Nazi chains.

The challenge to uncritical thinking and to uncriticized judgments little by little penetrated the theological schools, and still more slowly the pulpits, of Great Britain and the United States. Unitarianism was the chief organizational expression of the change. Wider in spread, but less definite in character, was that literary-critical approach to the Bible which was labeled 'modernism.' The essence of each was not opinion, for opinion varied widely among the personnel of both movements. The essence was attitude: the attitude of free enquiry, of research unhampered by taboos and unafraid of results, of scientific observation and scientific experiment.

The end is not yet; and among the lay public there has been little more than a beginning. The techniques are being learned, however, and the critical conscience is becoming aware of its own identity. Reverence for truth is rated above reverence for tradition as such. Not defence of what has been believed, but discovery of what can be, is the goal of honest religious scholarship. And honest scholarship is the first mark of the liberal approach to religious life.

Liberal scholarship, striving to be honest, learned ere long that final truth is difficult to reach and wellnigh impossible to define. Starting with a single ideal of enquiry, proceeding by identical techniques of observation and experiment, equally honest and equally able men arrived at judgments quite different and sometimes flatly contradictory. Being honest, none of them could assert that they were necessarily right and their dissenting *confrères* necessarily wrong.

The inevitable product of variety resulting from initial agreement was a new attitude of tolerance. If we *know* we are right, we may love the man who is wrong but we scarcely can respect his intellect. If we do not know we are right, we must admit some chance that we are wrong. Scholars differ, and we may reasonably expect that always they will. Liberal scholarship, allowing for a margin of error, can be neither contemptuous of difference nor belligerent toward the spokesmen of dissent. On this basis tolerance rises from the level of patronizing good will to the higher plane of mutual respect.

It is in this atmosphere of vitalized and purified tolerance that liberal religion has the advantage over other expressions of religious culture. Convinced of the final authority of the Church, the Catholic is precluded from enquiry beyond the limits which the Church has set; and consequently his good will toward other men, however warm, is limited by pity for their manifest errors. Asserting the verbal infallibility of the Bible, the Protestant fundamentalist must deny both the intellectual merit and the eternal salvation of those who reject his presuppositions. The liberal, knowing he may be wrong, credits to his intellectual opponents the possibility of their being right; and so he multiplies his chances of learning new truths for himself.

There is one quality of historic Jewish and Christian liberalism which goes beyond attitude and methodology into the zone of content. It is that of active human concern. This concern, so common among religious liberals as to be characteristic, springs directly from the considerations we have noticed. The give-and-take tolerance of the genuine liberal has led naturally toward appreciation of the dignity of all men. Research into the records of the Hebrew-Christian tradition has rediscovered, and has set newly in relief, that central place which the prophets in the Old Testament, the Gospels in the New, assigned to the worth of human personality.

It is not accidental that in our culture the Churches most influenced by critical scholarship are those most interested in social wellbeing. Authority sees men externally, tells them to stay put where now they are. 'Fundamentalism,' concerned with doctrines referred to a distant past and with diagrams of a distant future, inevitably tends to discount, if not wholly to ignore, man's life in the present. Liberalism, asserting the validity of the human mind and welcoming the phenomena of human difference, sees humanity as worthy of central and fully sympathetic valuation. The greatest practical gift which liberalism has given to our religious culture, up to date, is its conviction that the life of men and women in this world, the whole life of all men and women, is a matter of primary religious importance.

As we have found ourselves impelled to challenge some of the emphases of the earlier movements within the Hebrew-Christian tradition, we must notice now some dangers implicit in the liberal position, and some historic failures of the liberal approach. Valid as is the technique of enquiry, admirable as is the mood of tolerance, noble as is concern for humankind, each of these is peculiarly susceptible to subtle variations which if unchecked will make Christian liberalism effectively null and void.

The danger of objective enquiry is that it may lay so much weight upon technique as to become totally indifferent to result. Eager always to learn, the liberal is tempted always to question whether he has learned anything yet. Long ago it was remarked, by a shrewd analyst of current intellectual fashion, that some minds are so open that nothing whatever stays in them. The moral consequence is the point of real danger. Easily may we become so undecided as to what is true and right that we shall render no service to truth and right as now we see them.

We must be on guard against such stultification of our own spirits. We admit that we do not know the final answers. That does not excuse us from living, for the moment, by those tentative answers at which so far we have arrived. Perhaps we are wrong; and so perhaps, some time, we shall have to work very hard to tear down what now with painful labor we are building up. This is a chance we shall have to take, a chance with which always we must reckon. To taking that chance there is for the liberal no alternative but the dismal one of doing nothing.

Nothing is what so many liberals have done that they have brought discredit upon the entire liberal point of view. Uncertainty indeed may be a reason for inaction, but it is no sufficient excuse. The best which now we know, or which we think we know, is what we must live by until we find (as rightly the liberal may hope to find) something better still. Modern medicine is the end-product of scientific method in the laboratory; and without the practice of medicine the discoveries of the medical laboratory are meaningless. Useful living is the end-product of historical research and philosophical analysis; and without the practice of life, research and analysis are dead in themselves.

Akin to the menace of inaction attaching to enquiry is the danger of intellectual and moral casualness arising from tolerance. To admit that the other fellow may be right, that we may be wrong, sometimes encourages us to blur the lines between right and wrong altogether. Tolerance does not mean, and in intellectual integrity it must not mean, assent either to stupidity or to moral evil. Again, by the terms of the liberal approach, final judgment must be reserved. Again, by the urgency of the truly liberal spirit, working hypotheses must be followed to their proper consequences alike in logic and in conduct.

My light is mine, and yours is yours; and guided by differing lights we walk in varying paths. But my light still is mine, and by it only may I walk in hope of arriving somewhere. It is not permitted to me, whether in intellectual humility or in personal good will, to deny such light as I myself have seen. It is not required of me to pretend that for me my light is no better than is yours. Tolerance does not forbid argument. True tolerance, predicated on reverence for the truth itself, demands strenuous argument against what we think to be error, strenuous conflict with what we regard as being wrong. The liberal is tentative as to conclusions. There is no need, and there is no excuse, for his being sloppy as to thought or lazy as to action.

Human concern, again, slips oh! so readily into mere sentimentality. This has been clearly illustrated in the history of pacifism among religious liberals of our generation. Motivated by genuine good will toward all men, conditioned by a new mythology whose hobgoblins were diplomats and munitions-makers, the typical Christian college student of the 1920s and 1930s felt (the word is 'felt,' not 'thought') that war was the worst of all possible evils. He blinded himself therefore to the real complexities of international relations, deafened himself to the voices which were screaming hate and proclaiming destruction of the human spirit. Loving peace and loving folk, he forgot what people and politics really are like. Adopting good will as an attitude, he persuaded himself that good will was sufficient also as a technique.

Precisely similar has been the usual American liberal Christian approach to economics. Not the intricacies of the commodity and labor markets, but the spectacle of starving children and the spectre of overfed millionaires, held our attention. In any conflict between the 'haves' and 'have-nots' in the American community many of us were automatically and uncritically on the 'have-not' side. That was admirable as to spirit, and it may have been more often right than wrong as to economics; but seldom was it of any use. Not partisanship, but comprehension, is the prerequisite for social utility. Let us be concerned for justice; but let us implement that concern by learning how justice in practice can be made to work.

For vague good will in both economics and politics the true liberal must substitute precise knowledge and effective skill. Moral indifference he must reject in favor of moral urgency for the right as now he sees it. Intellectual fuzziness and practical indecision are forbidden to those whose primary canon is intellectual honesty. Liberalism is the natural product of our history, and, we may hope, the necessary framework of our future. Let us beware lest in us it disintegrate into casualness, indifferentism, fogginess, futility. Let us as liberals search for the truth in order to discover it; as liberals identify the right in order to contend for it; as liberals respect humankind in order to live significantly in and for it.

At that best which is legitimately its own, the liberal way is the path to ever widening vistas of knowledge, ever deepening treasuries of understanding, ever more valid techniques of action. Persons integral and whole, we shall be liberals in religion as in all of life. Among the materials we shall examine, and shall use in so far as we find them usable, are all the gifts that our past has given. It is our task as religious liberals clearly to see, accurately to measure, constructively to use, every element of our life. Our method is that of freedom: our goal is the truth. Our technique is to 'test all things': our hope is to 'hold fast the good.'

XIII

'WHAT MUST I DO TO BE SAVED?'

(The Revivalists)

'What must I do to be saved?'—Acts 16:30 (AV).

'Not many wise men after the flesh, not many mighty, not many noble.'—I Corinthians 1:26 (AV).

'Brethren, be not children in understanding.'
—I Corinthians 15:20 (AV).

THIS chapter, like that on the Methodists, stands where it does because actual chronological sequence is being maintained. Current revivalism, as represented in the 'Holiness' sects, and equally 'Fundamentalism' by that name and with its present characteristics, claim to represent primitive Christianity but do not. They are relatively recent developments, almost wholly peculiar to the American scene; and the personnel whom they attract are specially (and quite numerously) American. They are not older than liberal Christianity, but newer, for in their present form they constitute specifically a reaction against it.

It is of course true that the evangelist and the belligerent Biblical literalist can point to persons and to movements in the past that are to some extent precursors of themselves and of their activities. St. Paul may be said to have 'conducted a revival' in Thessalonica, the monastic orders followed the apostolic example in sending out wandering preachers, and almost all early Protestants professed belief in the inerrancy of the Scriptures. Nevertheless the 'mass revival' is chiefly American in its history, and in our day it has become the special mark (in intent if not always in achievement) of numerous small independent groups rather than an occasional activity of the larger Churches. Nor is it possible rightly to assign to such leaders as Martin Luther, John Wesley, or even John Calvin, any such naïve literalism in the handling of the Scriptures as has characterized the 'Fundamentalist' movement in the past quarter century.

American revivalism, including invariably a 'Fundamentalist' type of theology, derives from two dissimilar streams: from rigid Puritanism, and from the inchoate life of the frontier. The North American continent was settled just after the bitter religious conflicts of seventeenth-century England, and in part because of those conflicts. Many of the settlers brought with them a distrust of authority in general, and a hatred of Rome in particular, of which they were much more conscious than they were of any positive values either in their inherited or in their environmental faith. Their children, absorbing these attitudes, had access to still less of information. Eager nevertheless for something to which to cling, feeling especially in the rugged life of mountain and prairie the need of personal assurance, they grasped for such emotional satisfaction as they might be able to find.

This was available most readily in the briefer and (apparently) more easily understandable passages of the Scriptures. Thanks to Luther, Tyndale, and the scholars of Geneva, the Bible did go westward on the western march of man. The historic settings of the Biblical documents, acquaintance with which is so necessary to genuine understanding of meaning and to sound discrimination among values, were wholly unknown and therefore were totally ignored. 'Believe on the Lord Jesus Christ, and thou shalt be saved.' That sounded simple; and they who sought salvation chose devoutly to believe, though they scarcely could define on what. 'Without the shedding of blood there is no remission of sin.' That sounded simple too; and few read enough to notice that the context flatly forbids the application of this dictum to the Christian gospel.

The frontier forms of the historic Christian groups inevitably took on more and more of this eager and unreflective character, and came soon to regard it as normative Christianity. Urban Christianity meanwhile, still in touch with the outer world or renewing contact with it, moved slowly but surely in a progress that was rooted deeply and fruitfully in the authentic Hebrew-Christian past. Liberalism became standard in the seminaries, passed thence into the larger (and better-paying) pulpits, little by little has become familiar to laymen in the major denominations—if not always popular with them.

Always the countryside has had a profound distrust of the city, which it suspects (and not without reason) of arrogance, of trickiness, and often of immorality. The rural areas, and the host of city-dwellers recently transplanted from them and still rural in their attitudes and reactions, were disposed in any event to be antipathetic to the ways and ideas of the city Churches. When they saw crosses and candles, and robed clerics and choirs, they raised almost automatically the old protest against 'Romanism' which they had learned from their fathers. When they heard their assumptions for the first time challenged: a Biblical story treated as fiction, or salvation described in this-worldly and social terms rather than in heavenly and strictly individual: their feelings were deeply wounded, and their protests rose still more loudly.

Enough theological conservatism and enough acute Protestantism still survived among major denominational leaders, early in this century, to create a very real danger of a new series of splits across the whole American Christian pattern. 'The Christian Fundamentals League,' which originated the term 'Fundamentalism' and which in the name of simplicity promoted a complex if uninformed intellectualism, arose from a Presbyterian Church in full standing with its Presbytery. 'The Methodist League for Faith and Life,' which insisted on opinion and said little about conduct, was for a time supported by a few notable Methodist clerics as well as by a number of wealthy laymen. Most of this battle, so far as the larger Churches were concerned, was fought out to its real finish in the 1920s. There was no unconditional surrender; but liberalism held all the major seminaries, and now is more than ever characteristic of major denominational leadership.

Revivalism in its American pioneer form likewise has fought a losing contest within the urban Christian culture, and operates only on the fringes of metropolitan Church life. Anti-Catholicism was heavily discredited in the scandals that reduced the Ku Klux Klan to deliquescence. Where it exists today within 'standard' Protestantism, it has turned its attention almost wholly to the political activities of the Vatican in the international scene. Anti-ritualism is chiefly a regional matter; but the official recommendations of the Churches, as set forth in their various service books, have shown with each new edition a larger dependence upon historic forms of prayer and praise. Individualism persists as an American habit, but it has faced and is facing a thunderous barrage from the Federal Council of Churches and from the social action agencies of the several denominations.

Thus defeated in its effort to hold control of the older Christian institutions in this country, the frontier and agrarian type of Christianity has sought expression in new fellowships in which it might hope to rule unchallenged. The Church of the Nazarene was such a secession from Methodism, and one of the earliest of this kind: so early that already it is becoming a 'standard' denomination, and is drifting visibly if not rapidly toward standard liberalism. Most of the others are not so clearly derived from a single denominational source, but rather have gathered together the disaffected and the neglected from a variety of inherited official traditions.

Eighty-three per cent of the American membership in religious bodies is concentrated in twelve large units having more than a million members each, and ninety-five per cent in thirty-six Churches each with over one hundred thousand members. That leaves two hundred twenty denominations with a total of five per cent of American Church membership (two and a half million persons), averaging thus a little more than ten thousand members in each. Fourteen 'Churches of God' have just about a quarter million members among them, and nine 'Pentecostal' Churches count a total of less than sixty thousand. All told, some sixty-eight separate and independent denominations may be identified as wholly or dominantly of the revivalist type. Among them the sixty-eight have just over three quarters of a million members: not quite so many as are reported for the two major branches of Mormonism.

The rise and fall of the revivalist groups tend to be so rapid, their divisions and multiplications are so numerous, that it is not very significant to study them in terms of statistics. Few make any attempt to keep accurate records, and only occasionally is there real cohesion among any large number of local groups. The phenomenon is rather to be analyzed *ad hoc* wherever it appears, and is best understood in the light of the persisting conflict between farm and city, between the educationally underprivileged and the educationally advantaged.

It is easy for the educated city-dweller to point out the flaws and the fallacies in the movements which he is disposed to lump as 'Holy Roller outfits.' To begin with we have to allow for a certain amount of charlatanism, of outright dishonesty among the leaders. The very fact that the clientèle is unlettered and untrained, that it consists of 'children in understanding,' makes it an easy victim of appeals to prejudice, of glittering promises not payable in this world, of conjurations and scarcely veiled threats designed to collect the pennies of the penniless. Sinclair Lewis, who was something less than precise in his portrayal of the Baptist and Methodist Churches, in the revivalist episode of *Elmer Gantry* came close to exhibiting actual commercial revivalism at its actual worst.

Much more serious, because much more general, is the almost total disinterest of these sects in any present improvement of the social order. Their theology is both other-wordly and millennial, and so, despite the crying need of the people themselves, has no concern at all with wages and hours and conditions of life. It is by no accident that some men of wealth, who for their own reasons are greatly afraid of social change, have given generously to the support of Fundamentalist, revivalist, millennial movements and institutions. In this aspect, an unhappily common one, contemporary American revivalism has become indeed an opiate of the people.

The educational failure too is obvious. Despite the proud tradition of our American public schools, the average American is gravely suspicious of education and in particular of the educated. (Apart from religion, we may notice the controlling political view that professors of political science and of economics are by their very training disqualified from giving sound political and economic advice.) Many of the sects have made a positive virtue of ignorance, and devote much of their polemic to assaults on education. 'Bible Institutes,' professing to train for the ministry, offer admission to candidates who have 'an eighth grade education, or its equivalent.' Such self-conscious antipathy to learning augurs badly for the religious tutelage of many millions of Americans.

The writer is inclined, from personal observation, to discount heavily another charge often made against these groups: namely, that their emotional character leads into acute and illicit sexuality. Misbehavior and unwisdom in this realm are not unknown in other circles, and are readily induced by many factors quite different from 'the jerks' or 'the gift of tongues.' On the whole, such evidence as in reach suggests that the *mores* of the revivalists are scarcely less 'moral' than are those of their more sophisticated critics.

With all their faults and all their weaknesses, the revivalist sects are here. For a generation they have recruited in the cities adherents recently come from the countryside. For now more than a decade, with the migration of many thousands from the Southwest first to work in agriculture and then in war industries, they have been growing more and more prominent on the Pacific Coast. The Pentecostal Church, or some variant of it, was voted the place of special recognition in most of the Farm Security Administration camps for migratory workers. The Holiness Churches apparently are highly favored among the residents of the war housing projects. The city papers carry increasing numbers of advertisements headlined 'Great Revival!' or 'Bible Truth!' Is there any reason for the persistence of these movements, other than cultural lag? Does their presence stir in the contented Anglican, or Presbyterian, or Methodist, any reaction other than pity for these so deluded?

Granted that ignorance and suspicion and cultural inertia provide much of the explanation, it still behooves us to ask how it is that 'Apostolic Faith Missions' and 'Churches of God' gain so many hearers and apparently give to them so much of satisfaction. The first and principal answer is simply that the sects know how to meet the transplanted agrarian on his own level. This of course is to be condemned if it means, as sometimes it does, that a low level of knowledge and of religious experience is deliberately maintained and reënforced. It is rather to be admired, and perhaps to be emulated, in so far as it constitutes a direct and honest approach to people where and as they are.

The big Churches, with all their intelligence and decency, and with all the tremendous advantage of large and

well-equipped physical structures, have failed conspicu-
ously and lamentably to reach or really to serve the rural-
to-urban migrant. Part of the difficulty is simply that
middle class, semi-educated people are not genuinely interested in their social 'inferiors,' and are so ill at ease in
their presence that they make the newcomers themselves
hopelessly uncomfortable. Probably few of the clergy
have any such conscious feeling, and not many make griev-
ous errors in personal contacts. Often they have failed,
however, to bring to their settled urban congregations any
realization of immediate responsibility for the wellbeing
of people of strange habits, unfashionable clothes, and peculiar modes of speech. The 'Okies' simply are not welcome in most town and city Churches in California; and
they are not so insensitive as not to know it.

Even repentance for social snobbery will not be in itself
sufficient. No less needed is reformation in the use of
language. What the sects achieve that the Churches miss
is precisely that they speak in terms which their people
understand. Their grammar and pronunciation may be
lamentable, and if so need not be emulated. Their direct-
ness and simplicity is evident, and well may be studied and
imitated by those whose knowledge and training are superior. To no little extent it was not the actual content of
'modernism,' but rather its verbiage and its tone of voice,
that created so much fear and raised so much furor a generation ago. Spoken simply and honestly, phrased in terms
which the people themselves use, the message of a free and
creative Christianity need not remain unheard by simple
and honest folk. Polysyllables are useful, indeed inescap-
able, in the theological seminary. To translate them into
monosyllables, to apply them in life, should not be impos-

sible in view of the simple and direct nature of the Christian gospel in its own essence.

From personal observation the writer records another credit item for the revivalist groups. It is true that their ethical teaching is limited in scope because of the dominance of millennial expectations and of primary interest in individual escape from eternal punishment. It may be, also, that the highly intellectualist emphasis which Fundamentalism has given to 'faith' has tended to sacrifice concern for conduct to interest in opinion. It is not true, however, that all the sects are indifferent to personal moral character in immediate personal relationships. There is in much of their preaching a pronounced ethical note, proclaimed with driving emphasis and urged sharply upon each individual hearer. Such *ad hominem* preaching no doubt might be embarrassing in many of the 'respectable' Churches; but it might not be altogether unhealthy. We need not cease to try to understand the universe, to try to explain what we think we have understood. We shall profit by adding, and with positive conviction, some recognition of the claims of Christian faith upon the personal behavior of the faithful.

Finally, we shall do well to ask ourselves again the question which was raised in our enquiry into religious liberalism: the question of active devotion. The sects could not survive were not the majority of leaders and members genuinely sincere, vitally enthusiastic. They care about their religion, care enough to give to it and to live for it. We have little right to feel superior to them so long as to a more historic and better considered faith we accord so much less than our own full measure of devotion. The revivalist may be wrong in thinking that dignity and order are signs of indifference in themselves. He is unquestionably right in charging that indifference marks many of our most dignified and orderly Churches.

The one effective competitor with the sects, among all the historic Churches, is the Church of Rome. It draws most of its American adherents, obviously, from groups of European Catholic background. It holds them, however, because along with the sects it welcomes people without social classification; because it has mastered the art of direct and simple teaching; because it insists on specific canons of behavior; and most of all because it has absolute faith in its own mission. It does all this without compromising either its intellectual position or its usages in worship: a point which we Protestants well may note. The Catholic Church and the sects usually and enthusiastically condemn each other. Nevertheless they both succeed because they have substantially the same approach to people and use substantially the same methods in dealing with them.

The success of the Catholic Church in reaching the working classes, along with that of Lutheranism in holding the allegiance of agrarian Scandinavians, indicates that antipathy to ritualism does not necessarily characterize all the 'common people' as such. It does belong to many inheritors of the English Puritan tradition, and in them manifestly is not going to disappear overnight. Ritual has no justification, in any event, except as it provides 'outward and visible signs of inward and spiritual grace.' It is probable that gradual adjustment to urban ways, and increasing and friendly contact with members of the 'ritualist' groups, will lead some of the pronounced anti-ritualists to revalue their values. Meanwhile, and probably always, room must be left for the expression of a variety of individual and group preferences in this instrumental aspect of religious life.

They who believe that the sects do not supply adequately the total religious needs of mankind must decide whether they themselves propose primarily to compete with the sects as institutions or to serve their members as people. Some competition there will be, and rightly; for each of us is justified in wishing to share with others the values that he himself has found good. But valid competition must be competition in usefulness, and by no means a matter of mere deprecation or condemnation of what we deem inadequate modes of religious expression. Many people are children in understanding, and we do well to hope that they may become adult. We can help them toward adulthood not by contempt for their childishness, but only by direct and sympathetic and simple teaching.

The real choice of the future is not between historic Christianity and the aberrant sects, but rather between a living Christianity and an unrelieved secularism. The rural religious pattern will not long be maintained as its representatives and their children become naturalized into urban life. As things now stand, a very few of these will grow into the mood and manner of the urban Churches. The vast majority, learning in time that revivalism does not meet the issues nor solve the problems of metropolitan experience, will abandon such religion as they have, without thinking to find a replacement more adequate. At this point the taverns and the professionally anti-religious leftists will be the really effective contenders for the time and the personal allegiance of those who have lost their former anchorage. If this is not to be, the Churches will have to rethink, readjust, and revitalize both their teaching and their practice.

What shall we do to be saved, not as institutions but as profitable servants? The answer actually is nothing other than the carrying through of the truly liberal Christian attitude into free and abundant service; and this, oddly enough, is identical with the best that the sects themselves have achieved. It means genuine, personal concern for humankind. It requires simple utterance. It involves a stirring and stringent challenge to the moral will of men and women. Above and beyond all, it demands of the privileged that they shall be no less sincere, no less eager, no less devoted, than the underprivileged have been. If the Churches can and will meet these requirements (and they can if they will) they will lead many from childishness of understanding into maturity of experience. But some of the 'children in understanding' will have shown them how to do it.

XIV

'ONE BODY IN CHRIST'

(The Hebrew-Christian Tradition)

> *'As the body is one, and hath many members, and all the members of that one body, being many, are one body: so also is Christ.'*—I Corinthians 12:12 (AV).

> *'I am come that they might have life, and that they might have it more abundantly.'*—St. John 10:10 (AV).

A very real danger inheres in such a study as up to this point we have pursued. The consequence of a chronologically arranged enquiry very easily may be negation, as factor by factor the past seems to lose its relevance to the present. The Catholic Church repudiated Judaism, the Protestant movement denied Catholicism, the liberal and revivalist moods rejected contrasting aspects of Protestantism. Confessedly we have found both historic liberalism and current revivalism imperfect. What then have we left?

Ere we ask ourselves some concluding questions about the Church that is to be, we shall do wisely to pause and consider the positive character of the Church that still and now is. In point of fact the successive denials made by the new movements and new institutions we have studied have been principally forensic and polemic. They have not been in any final way, nor even to any large degree, implemented in cultural fact. Jewish values survived in Cathol-icism, Catholic symbols and teachings in Protestantism, Protestant attitudes of varying sorts in liberalism and re-vivalism. Nor is it possible to believe that the older insti-tutions, each in its turn, have remained untouched and uninfluenced by younger ways of thinking and of behav-ing.

The truth about our religious culture is that all of us continue to be Jewish, and Orthodox, and Catholic, and Protestant, and liberal; and so that each of us is more than any one, more than all of these if taken separately. Not a mere total, but an organic synthesis, is the fruit of our his-tory and the subject of our enquiry. Our religious heritage remains one more truly than it has become many; and its whole is greater and truer than is the sum of its parts.

In sum, we are Christian. But what does 'Christian' mean? Strictly speaking, since the Greek word *Christos* is a literal translation of the Jewish term 'Messiah,' 'the anointed,' 'Christianity' should mean 'Messianism' and a 'Christian' should be identified as a 'Messianist.' Histor-ically this is manifest nonsense. Early Christianity was Messianic, and could be, only by rejecting every familiar Jewish concept of the Messiah's function (which was highly nationalistic and most usually military, with or without supernatural involvements). In passing we should note that Judaism itself has been Messianic only in part, and decreasingly through the years. When the Christian Church became assimilated to Greco-Roman culture it dis-carded what little of Jewish Messianism it ever had main-tained. The word 'Christ' lost all significance as a title, and became what it is for us: a name without initial meaning.

'Without initial meaning'? The important thing for us to realize is that 'Christian' has had a very real and very great acquired meaning, in terms of the total religious culture of the western world. Traditionally the point of reference still is Jesus of Nazareth. Historically, effectively, the integrating factor is not one life in ancient Palestine, but the interplay of countless lives through nineteen centuries of western history. To be a 'Christian' now is something very different from: and, through the enriching gifts of time, can be something very much greater than: to be a 'Christian' when first the designation was used in ancient Antioch.

We have given no attention in this little book to the other great religious traditions of mankind: the Hindu, the Buddhist, the Confucian, the Muslim. This is not because they are unimportant, nor because they have nothing to contribute. It is altogether probable that in a new world culture we may hope to gain much from acquaintance with them and perhaps by a measure of participation in them. To date, however, we have been little influenced by the non-Christian faiths, and culturally we remain outside their field.

Where we are is within the area of the Christian (which is, as we have seen, the Hebrew-Christian) tradition. The framework and the constituents of our thought are Jewish, Greek, Roman, mediaeval, Renaissance, modern European, recent American. These are the cultures which are built into our thinking and our feeling; and these cultures unite in one organism only: in the organic, living, functioning reality into which we were born, the society and the scheme of values called 'Christian.'

Being organic, the Christian culture has been dynamic. The weakness and the ultimate falsity of unyielding traditionalism lie in the effort to equate Christianity with the situations of various selected points in past time: whether in the first century, in pre-Renaissance Europe, in the Lutheran revolt, or in the Methodist revival. Christianity indeed includes these: but all of these, and much more beside. Christianity is also Greek metaphysics and Roman law and English nationalism and German Biblical scholarship. It is also monasticism and Lollardry, ritualism and Quakerism, the Papacy and the Kentucky evangelist. It is Rabbi Ben Ezra, and Chaucer's parson, and Erasmus and Savonarola. It is St. Paul and St. Augustine, it is St. Francis and St. Thomas More, it is Mary Doe and Richard Roe.

The structure of the preceding paragraph is one of contrasts: deliberately so at this point, for contrast is integral to the pattern that we are trying to see. We have noted, from chapter to chapter, how each new trend filled gaps left by its precursors, how each attempted to balance overemphases prevalent when it arose. Greek and Roman Catholicism supplied what Judaism never had attempted, an inclusive philosophical framework within which the details of faith and life became coherently related. Protestantism challenged the too great claims of authority, made room for the life of the individual. Liberalism has rejected the Protestant inclination to emotionalize dogma, has sought to emphasize upbuilding rather than protest *per se*. Revivalism challenges the liberal disposition to be indifferent as to persons and as to values.

At the same time the continuity of Christian thought and life is demonstrated again and again as we trace the threads down through the years. The Jewish demand for social justice is echoed in the Catholic community and in the liberal concern for human welfare. The priestly ritual of Judaism is reflected in Catholic order and most recently in a revival of symbolic and ceremonial interest in the liberal Churches. Jewish devotion reappears in Protestant intensity of faith and in revivalist enthusiasm. Catholic theology was taken over almost as a whole by Protestantism, while the active intellectual curiosity out of which the theology arose is revived in the liberal eagerness to enquire. Protestant Biblicism laid the foundations not only for Fundamentalist dogma but also for liberal Biblical study. Thus each item of the past reappears in a new present, and each item of our present is based upon our past.

Nor is our unity historical only. Consisting as it does of interwoven strands, of interpenetrating concepts and needs, it consists vitally in and about a center which the word 'Christian' has come to connote. 'Christianity,' we have seen, is other than the Messianism which etymologically it ought to be. Is it possible for us to identify the focal point of Hebrew-Christian faith and life?

Despite what has been said negatively about terminology, the center is to be found precisely in the concept represented by 'the Christ.' Not as Messiah, apocalyptic or military; not as Jesus of Nazareth, about whom we know so little that we should refrain from guessing at all; not only as the Second Person of the orthodox Trinity (though that aspect is more nearly relevant for us than are the others); not in these terms, but in the historic and central concept of incarnation, 'the Christ' is the veritable, vital center of the Christian pattern.

In a paper recently presented before the Pacific Coast

Theological Group, Dr. E. Van N. Diller of Mills College pointed out that a genuine statement of incarnation appears in the earliest Jewish legend of the first human being. 'And the Lord God formed man,' says the ninth century Judean folk-tale, 'of the dust of the ground, and breathed into his nostrils the breath of life; and man became a living soul.' That is to say, and without any improper wresting of the meaning, that man is alive only as the spirit of God is in him; which is to say, again, that the spirit of God is the very life of man.

The phenomena of human experience have made that doctrine sometimes very difficult to believe. Judging by the behavior of some people: sometimes one thinks of most people: it might be contended that not the spirit of God, but the spirit of the devil, is the vitalizing factor in human affairs. Consequently men soon began to make distinctions, to conclude that the divine life was much more definitely and more recognizably present in some lives than it was in others. At least in some phases of the Jewish Messianic tradition, the Messiah was regarded as being possessed in special degree of the divine spirit. Thus an anonymous passage now embedded in our book of Isaiah:

The spirit of the Lord shall rest upon him, the spirit of wisdom and understanding, the spirit of counsel and might, the spirit of knowledge and of the fear of the Lord.

It is not surprising that the early Christians assigned to Jesus precisely this quality, and accounted for it on substantially the same grounds. They had available also, and from the time of the writing of the Fourth Gospel explicitly used, the Stoic concept of the *logos spermaticos*, the 'generative Word,' the divine light and power permeating and vitalizing all the constituents of the world order. Historic Christianity held and taught that the *logos* became man most fully in Jesus of Nazareth; and using the Greek word translating (but in actual Greek Christian usage not duplicating) the old Jewish title, it said that 'Jesus is the Christ.'

It must be emphasized, however, that it is 'the Christ,' and not the historic Jesus of Nazareth, who is the central value of the Christian faith. Not a series of episodes in first-century Palestine, but a continuity of experience throughout the centuries, gave reality to the conviction that God indeed might be found in the life of man. This continuity, and this resultant conviction, are the essence of the Christian way, of Christian teaching, of the Christian scale of values. Christianity is the affirmation that God may be known to man because God can be found in man. To this affirmation every Christian, Jewish and Catholic and Protestant and liberal, gives his hearty and cardinal assent.

To have life, to have it ever more abundantly, is the gift of the Christian revelation. This not only permits change, and even conflict: it demands them, as life must change and therefore must contend. This allows for difference, for life knows difference as the condition necessary to growth. This requires delimitation of relative values, recognition of positive gains and healthy losses. This finds room both for discipline and for enquiry, for community and for individuality, for institutional fidelity and for wide-reaching social concern. All this is living; and Christianity holds that, being living, it is divine; and being divine, it may be, can be, is, found and experienced in all that is human.

It is for these reasons that each of our four Gospels gives us a different portrait of Jesus, that each generation has presented 'the Christ' as the summation of the best that it has known and dreamed. A striking symbolism is provided in the Fourth Gospel, where Mary of Magdala is said to have looked in vain into the tomb of Jesus. At last she gave up; and then the revelation burst upon her: the revelation of the living Christ close by, walking with her in the garden in which she had been all the time. The tombs of the past are worth our investigating; but the life of the present is where chiefly we must live. In the life of the present we must seek, in the life of the present we shall find, both the sources and the substance of our living faith.

Now and then historic Christianity has failed of its own mission by devoting too much attention to the asserted phenomena of the Gospel story. When it has done this it has driven away its Jewish comrades, has created friction among its greatest thinkers, has bewildered its humble adherents, has denied its own central meaning. When it has arisen above the phenomena to search for the ultimate ideal: and when thereupon it has been able to discern the ideal reflected not only in the selected events of thirty years, but also in all the phenomena of all of human living: then Christianity has been Christian indeed.

We American Christians are Jewish: for we have found the divine in simple humanity, in reverent worship in unquenchable loyalty. We are Catholic: for we have found the divine in community, in universality, in discipline. We are Protestant: for we have found the divine in individuality, in the glorious records of the past, in the intensity of our own devotion. We are liberal: for we have found the divine in the quest for truth, in humility as to our own achievements, in eager concern for our fellows. We are then Christian: for in all of these we have found, and have known, and have lived in, the Christ. We have lived in the living Christ discerned as the center of the Christian hope. We have found life in the Christ of incarnation, the Christ which is God in the life of man.

XV

'DECENTLY AND IN ORDER'

(The Church of the Future)

> 'Let all things be done decently and in order.'
> —I Corinthians 14:40 (AV).
>
> 'Endeavouring to keep the unity of the spirit in the bond of peace.'—Ephesians 4:3 (AV).
>
> 'In essentials, unity; in non-essentials, liberty; in all things, charity.'—Commonly ascribed to Philip Melanchthon, A.D. 1497–1560; by Canon Farrar assigned to 'Rupertus Meldinius' (Robert of Melun, A.D. 1100–1167, Bishop of Hereford?).

'LET all things be done decently and in order.' This advice, which St. Paul wrote to his somewhat disorderly friends in Corinth with special reference to what went on in their gatherings for worship, always has been worth offering to all the Church as to all the aspects of its thought and life. Decency and order are not incompatible with enthusiasm, as witness the very fact that the injunction comes to us from the enthusiastic St. Paul himself. Decency and order are necessary if enthusiasm is to be efficient, if faith is to express itself powerfully in life. And so it is on this practical and rather quiet note that our present study comes to its close.

There is no use pretending, in the light of what we have

observed, that the Church's conduct always has been decent and orderly. Often its mood has been contentious, its thinking confused, its behavior highly erratic. Sometimes its very eagerness has produced a disorder which has meant ineffectiveness. But we may reasonably judge that decency and order usually have been sought, if not always found; and we may reasonably believe that the Church of today gives increasing promise of living a decent, orderly, and effective life.

It shows signs, to begin with, of growing decency and order in its thinking. Not always has this been true of the Church. In the eyes of his own generation John Wesley was a revolutionary when he declared that 'Opinion is not religion; not even right opinion.' Through the centuries the western world (often the Orient has felt and spoken otherwise) has tended in all realms to emphasize opinion as crucial; and disagreements among Christians as to what was right opinion have led not only to dispute but also to violence and death.

Oddly enough, once we set aside the notion that opinion as such is of primary importance, we are much the more likely to find ourselves moving toward the discovery of opinions that really are tenable and defensible. The stubborn guarding of a single intellectual position, inherited or acquired, does little to help us see it clearly or evaluate it thoughtfully. If, however, we conclude that our eternal salvation does not depend on our maintaining those views which now we hold, we are set free to the kind of intellectual enquiry and adventure that may bring us nearer to the truth that is.

Most of the theological controversies of the past no

longer stir American Christians very deeply. Perhaps it is unfortunate that so few Presbyterians know that Calvin stood for determinism, so few Methodists that Wesley contended for free will; but it is well that Presbyterians and Methodists no longer sever friendships nor call names because they cannot agree about the teachings of Arminius. We may wish that more people knew what the Unitarians have contributed to the development of modern Christian thinking; but we may be grateful that so many people unconsciously, and without any sort of inner conflict, have absorbed so much of Unitarian honesty and have used it in the operating of their own minds.

There was indeed a recrudescence of formal and belligerent intellectualism in the American Protestant scene a generation ago, in the Fundamentalist movement. Here it was insisted that right opinion was at the very heart of Christianity, and moreover that the only right opinions were those held by the leaders of that particular group: opinions expressed first in five specific points, and then (inevitably in such a thought pattern) stated with four more points added, to make a total of nine.

Fundamentalism stirred up some excitement, gained adherents among the uncritical and uninformed, caused the division of a very few local Churches and of one important theological school. It succeeded in gaining control of no major Protestant denomination. Two decades ago an outspokenly Fundamentalist journal published a list of the few theological seminaries in the country that it considered doctrinally safe and sound. Among them was no single official school of the Episcopal, the Presbyterian, the Congregational, the Methodist, or the Baptist Churches. Today the warfare which raged between 'Fundamentalists' and 'modernists' is forgotten by the mass of American Christians; few young people of our time ever have heard of it; and the attempt to identify true religion with a specific theological pattern may be regarded as having failed.

A liberal intellectual attitude, we have noticed, makes it possible for one to learn more readily and more adequately. It is no less true that accurate learning in the religious field inevitably develops liberalism in attitude. To trace the course of theological discussion through the centuries is to recognize how many magnificent persons have been magnificently wrong, to be driven to admit that often there is little ground for absolute choice between two opposing ideas, to realize that very much of our enquiry into the nature of things still goes out into impenetrable mystery. This does not excuse us from further enquiry; rather it forbids our supposing that enquiry ever may be suspended.

Not claiming to know so much as some of the fathers thought they knew, and thereby liberated to learn more than is known at present, the Churches of our time differ less and less one from another in the realm of ideas. There are liberals and conservatives in every denomination. There are voluntarist Presbyterians and determinist Methodists. There are in all Churches all shades of judgment about the nature of the divine incarnation in Jesus Christ. There is above all a continuing freedom of enquiry, a growing freedom of discussion; and the more room we have made for variation within a given fellowship, the more nearly we have found all our fellowships drawn together.

Decency and order in the realm of ideas mean simply the application of scientific method, the maintaining of the mood of scientific enquiry. This method the Churches, along with the world, have been learning more and more; this liberal mood they are holding. The Church of the future we may rightly expect to be intellectually respectable because intellectually honest; and therefore decent and orderly in its talking as in its thinking.

St. Paul's specific point in urging 'decency and order' upon the Corinthians was that of conduct in the service of worship. Here the Anglican Churches have the clearest record among the Protestant groups, though even they have had their times of uncertainty and confusion. Puritanism, gravely troubled by what it regarded as the substituting of ritual for religion, jumped to the conclusion that it could promote true religion by destroying ritual. American Protestantism, Puritan in much of its heritage and pioneer in its cultural setting, went to the extreme of disorder and haphazardness in its usages of worship, and often sought to make a virtue out of wilful carelessness.

We are beginning now to emerge from the frontier. In practically every major Protestant denomination there is an unmistakable trend toward what is called 'ritualism.' In large measure this grows directly out of an increasingly objective study of the past, with a consequently enlarged appreciation of what the past has given us. There is also a richer understanding of the human need for beauty and the human capacity to respond to it. Of course one can be religious without crosses and candles, one can pray in one's own words and without kneeling, one can speak deep spiritual truth while wearing a business suit. But it is true also that the symbols have helped and do help many people, that the words of long ago can speak directly and profoundly to us of today, that attitude of body may reflect and may affect attitudes of mind and heart, that dignity of presentation is not inconsistent with honesty of thought.

We need not expect, and we shall not have, complete uniformity in the forms of our Church services. It is a striking fact that many Episcopalians turn Quaker, and many Quakers Episcopalian: a striking fact, but not at all a puzzling one. Culturally the two groups have much in common. Both are principally English in background. Both belong historically to the earlier settlements in this country. Both represent much the same social strata, and share much the same assumptions of moral value. The point on which their traditions differ sharply is that of the preferable kind of ritual. (As was noted above, the Quakers have a ritual no less than do the Anglicans. The contrast is one simply of the kind of ritual, between the sparse and possibly spontaneous on the one hand, the elaborate and predetermined on the other.) When a Quaker finds the silent meeting bare, he turns Episcopalian. When an Episcopalian finds the Order for the Holy Communion turgid, he turns Quaker. This is by all means as it should be, and it may be hoped that transfers of this entirely reasonable sort will continue.

Meanwhile the dominant tendency in Protestant worship is toward more careful planning of the service, and toward the elaboration of its details of decoration, movement, and utterance. Especially if this goes with thoughtful preparation of the sermon, so that the preacher's claiming of so much of the congregation's time becomes other than unmitigated impertinence, we may well be thankful. (One recalls the remark attributed to an Anglican Bishop, to the effect that 'When the Holy Ghost speaks extempore, he usually talks nonsense.') Beauty, dignity, decency, order: these we seek in the service thoughtfully prepared and reverently conducted. These we may expect the Church of the future to continue, and further to nourish.

If we are to have unity in essentials, we shall have to begin by asking whether we can agree as to what the essentials are. Identity of opinion we have seen to be impossible, and opinion therefore to be a field for liberty rather than one for required uniformity. Identity of our forms of worship cannot be enforced because both our abilities and our preferences vary, and any attempt to require a single formula is sure to break down. We can get along with widely varying ideas, and we can get along with highly varying types of Church service: we can get along with them, and for the enriching of our experience we need them. Is there yet a field for unity, a field of essentials in which it is essential that we be united?

For our present purposes the question of organizational unity may be dropped almost as quickly as it is raised. The several branches of the major denominations show increasing eagerness to get together, and such a trend is to be welcomed. The unifying of various denominations into a single Church is something much more difficult to achieve in a culture so complex as is ours: Canada did wisely to finish the job while she was young, sparsely populated, and relatively homogeneous. Basically, it is not union of structures but unity of spirit that we need; and this brings us to the prime essentials.

There is a field of essential unity; or perhaps there are two fields, closely related to and dependent upon each other. We must seek unity, for we need unity, in the realms of attitude and of action: of attitude leading to action, of action springing from attitude. The secret of unity in these essentials is rooted in the Hebrew-Christian faith in incarnation, in the discovery of the divine in human life. The secret of unity flowers in the last phrase of the saying prefixed to this chapter: *In omnibus, caritas:* 'in all things, charity'—'in all things, good will.'

Good will toward men, predicated upon God's incarnation in man, is the central theme of the Christian message. It is the Christian criterion of value, the Christian motive for conduct, the Christian solvent for problems. Lacking good will, the Church quarreled and divided over ideas and structures and forms of worship. Making good will secondary to Churchly authority, Queen Mary's advisers burned Latimer and Ridley and Cranmer. Making good will secondary to Puritan reforming, the English Commonwealth executed Archbishop Laud. Making good will secondary to accepted patterns, Boston expelled Roger Williams and Anne Hutchinson, hanged four Quakers on the Common.

It is a sorry story as we tell it over, and it is a story in which no one's hands are clean. Happily we may believe that we know better now, and will do better. Christian good will, keeping the unity of the spirit in the bond of peace, has been more nearly effective within the Church of our times than it was in that of the sixteenth and seventeenth centuries. To some extent we have learned to love our brothers, to love even those brothers whom we do not fully resemble nor quite understand. To that extent we have apprehended the gospel of the incarnation, of the living God in the life of man; and so to that extent we are Christian.

But we have yet a long way to go. Within the Church, institutional interests still keep apart some organizations which have every good reason for being together. The Methodists divided over slavery in 1844, and did not get together until 1940. The Presbyterians and Baptists, dividing for the same reason, are not united yet. (One cannot avoid the recognition that here, as at so many other points, the Churches very clearly reproduce the behavior pattern of all human institutions.) The Federal Council of Churches of Christ in America has not yet admitted the Unitarians within its pale of fellowship, though many of the Council's own leaders are close to being Unitarian in their personal thinking; while on the other hand some groups abjure what they consider the heresies of the Federal Council. The revivalists still condemn city Christianity, and the urban Churches look down upon the naïve agrarians.

What is infinitely more serious is the pitifully small impact which to date the Church has made upon the world at large in the affecting of that world by its vitalizing spirit of good will toward and among men. We have not solved the problems of economic rapacity, of interracial conflict, of the vast social disorganization that is war. We need intelligence in the meeting of these problems: economic good sense, social understanding, political wisdom. But we need good will as well, and not less; and hitherto we have not successfully made the case for good will either by precept or in example.

Yet it must be recognized that among human organizations none in our time has outranked the Church in earnest effort in this direction, that none has surpassed it in success. The Quaker witness for peace has gone far toward revolutionizing not only Christian thinking about war, but also the thinking of all mankind. The cause of decency and order in industrial relationships has been advanced far by the social action programs of the Churches. Perhaps the passing of resolutions avails little, but the Churches have added achievement to their resolving. We may not forget, for example, the notable and determining part played in the reorganization of employment practices in the steel industry by the report of the Interchurch World Movement on the steel strike of 1920.

When ten years ago, in California, free speech and free assembly were effectively denied in public hysteria over labor relations, the writer found that he had freedom to speak for freedom in Church after Church, when not only lodge halls but also public school and even college buildings were firmly closed to him. (Few names of living persons have been mentioned in these pages; but it is eminently proper to record here the Christian graciousness and Christian courage, in those strenuous days, of the Right Reverend Edward L. Parsons, Protestant Episcopal Bishop of California; of Dr. Oswald W. S. McCall of the First Congregational Church in Berkeley; and of Dr. Edgar Allan Lowther of Temple Methodist Church in San Francisco.) Perhaps the finest statement made on the recent and bitter controversy over Negro membership in the Boilermakers' Union was issued by the San Francisco chapter of the Association of Catholic Trade Unionists. Today none are speaking out more clearly, more bravely, for rational treatment of Americans of Japanese ancestry, than are Christian leaders both lay and ministerial.

There is reason for doubt as to the wisdom of active participation by the Church, as an organization, in specific political action either for the election of candidates or for the enactment of laws. Here the possible margin of error is so great that it is impossible to say that a single party or a single program is so right that every Christian must needs support it. But religion is concerned with all of human life, and therefore the religious society which is the Church must enquire into, must discuss, everything that touches life at any point. Further, the individual Christian, motivated by good will, is obligated to express that good will in vigorous support of every program that his judgment tells him points toward human wellbeing, in courageous assault upon every proposal that he regards as harmful to his fellow men. The proper function of the Church here is to provide accurate data on issues, a frame of moral reference, opportunity for free and honest discussion, above all warm encouragement to clear personal thinking and devoted personal action.

The divisions of an army bear different designations and wear different emblems. Often they perform different and highly specialized tasks. But they serve together, they fight together against a common enemy and toward the one goal of common victory. The army that is the Church of Jesus Christ is one drawn from all the miscellany of humankind, and each division of it has its own proud traditions and its own special qualities.

We belong to one division or to another as we may have been recruited, or as we may have chosen to enlist. A few of us may decide to seek reassignment to another division, because we think we belong more naturally to it and therefore shall serve more effectively in its ranks.

That is a secondary matter. The important thing is that we are all in the same army. We fight against the same foemen: hate, and cruelty, and evil in its every form. We seek to obey the same commands of love to God and love to fellow man. Within our forces we endeavour to hold the unity of the spirit in the bond of peace.

Knowing this, believing in it, living by it, we rejoice as we hear the battle-cry of each advancing unit of our forces. With the revivalists we seek for man's saving from sin. With the liberals we 'test all things,' to the end that we may 'hold fast the good.' With Alexander Campbell we speak what we are persuaded is the truth, keep silent when we know we do not know. With Wesley we ask, 'Is thine heart right?' and with him we answer, 'If it be, give me thy hand.' 'In this Silence,' with Woolman, 'we learn abiding in the Divine Will.' With the Elkhorn Baptists we see believers as the subjects of the divine command, and with Carey and Judson all men as objects of the divine concern. With Milton we hold that Truth never is 'put to the worse in a free and open encounter.' With the Anglicans we pray 'for the whole state of Christ's Church.' With the Presbyterians we seek to glorify God in the doing of his will. With Luther we cry, 'Here we stand. God helping us, we can no other.'

With the Catholic we seek the saving grace that lives in community. With the Orthodox we labor to discover and to define the truth. With the Jews we pledge our allegiance to the one Lord who is theirs and ours, the Lord to whom first they introduced us. With every sharer in the Hebrew-Christian tradition we look toward the Christ who is God incarnate in humanity.

Like a mighty army moves the Church of God;
Brothers, we are treading where the saints have trod;
We are not divided, all one body we,
One in hope and doctrine, one in charity.

A young Anglican clergyman in Yorkshire wrote that for a children's processional eighty years ago, and the worldwide Church has been singing it ever since. God grant that the Church ever may live it: united in the essential, free in the incidental, compelled by good will in all. Decently and in order we go forward, keeping the unity of the spirit in the bond of peace.

INDEX

THE MACMILLAN COMPANY
NEW YORK · BOSTON · CHICAGO
DALLAS · ATLANTA · SAN FRANCISCO

MACMILLAN AND CO., LIMITED
LONDON · BOMBAY · CALCUTTA
MADRAS · MELBOURNE

**THE MACMILLAN COMPANY
OF CANADA, LIMITED**
TORONTO